INTERNATIONAL ASSOCIATION FOR THE EVALUATION
OF EDUCATIONAL ACHIEVEMENT (IEA)

IEA Monograph Studies No. 6

Tolerating Political Dissent

The Impact of High School Social Climates in the United States and West Germany

H. Dean Nielsen
Stanford University
and
University of Stockholm

Almqvist & Wiksell International
Stockholm

© H. Dean Nielsen, 1977

All rights reserved

Printed in Sweden by
TEXTgruppen i Uppsala AB, 1977

ISBN 91-22-00118-2

Table of Contents

	Page
ACKNOWLEDGEMENTS	9
ABSTRACT	11

CHAPTER

1. SOCIAL CONFLICT AND DISSENT TOLERATION 13
   Introduction 13
   The Role of Social Conflict in Democracies 14
   Coping with Social Conflict 16
   The Socialization of Dissent Toleration 19
   Dissent Toleration in the United States 20
   Dissent Toleration in the Federal Republic of Germany 22
   Summary 23

2. FORMAL EDUCATION AND DISSENT TOLERATION 24
   Introduction 24
   The Impact of Formal Education 25
   School Social Climate and Dissent Toleration 25
   Political Cognitions and Dissent Toleration 29
   Conditioners of the Influence of Schooling 30
       Antecedent Conditions 30
       Concurrent Conditions 31
       Anticipatory Conditions 32
   The Analytical Model 33
   Hypothesis Formulation 33

3. THE IEA DATA SET 35
   IEA as a Research Enterprise 35
   The IEA Civic Education Data 35
   Development of Research Instruments 37
       Cognitive Instruments 37
       Attitudinal Instruments 37
       Background Information 39
   Sampling in the Two Countries 39
   Collection and Treatment of the Data 43
   Summary 44

4. MEASUREMENT OF THE VARIABLES 45
   Operationalizing Dissent Toleration 46
      Choosing the Appropriate Indicators 46
      Constructing the Dissent Toleration Scale 47
   Operationalizing School Social Climate 49
      Dimensions of Social Climate 49
      Constructing Subscales 56
      Choosing Items 57
      Constructing the School Social Climate Scales 58
   Operationalizing the Conditioning Variables 61
      Antecedent Conditions 61
      Concurrent Conditions 62
      Anticipatory Conditions 62
   Measuring Civics Knowledge 62
   Summary 63

5. THE ANALYSES 64
   Preliminary Considerations 64
      Unit of Analysis 65
      Between Country Comparisons 66
   Descriptive Statistics 67
   Zero-Order Correlations with Dissent Toleration 69
   Zero-Order Correlations with Civics Knowledge 71
   Zero-Order Correlations with the Conditioning Variables 74
   Multiple Regression Analysis 76
   Contextual Analysis 79
   Disaggregating the Effects of School Social Climate 83
   Regression Analysis by Type of Program for the Federal
      Republic of Germany 87
   Path Analysis 89
   Summary of Results 94

6. SUMMARY AND CONCLUSIONS 97
   General Findings 98
   Specific Findings for the United States 101
   Specific Findings for the Federal Republic of Germany 102
   Educational Policy Implications 105
   Concluding Remarks 109

APPENDIX 111

BIBLIOGRAPHY 133

List of Figures, Exhibits and Tables

Page

FIGURES
1.1 The General Socialization Model 21
2.1 The Theoretical Model 29
2.2 The Analytical Model 33
5.1 Zero-Order Relationships Between School Social Climate, Civics Knowledge and Dissent Toleration 74
5.2 Relationships between School Social Climate, Civics Knowledge and Dissent Toleration Controlling for Conditioning Variables 79
5.3 Relationships Between School Social Climate, Civics Knowledge and Dissent Toleration in Contextual Analysis 83
5.4 Standardized Regression Coefficients for the Relationships between Social Climate Variables and Dissent Toleration Controlling for Conditioning Variables—USA and FRG 85
5.5 Standardized Regression Coefficients for the Relationships between Social Climate Variables and Civics Knowledge Controlling for Conditioning Variables—USA and FRG 86
5.6 Basic Path Model—USA and FRG 91
5.7 Expanded Path Model—USA and FRG 93

EXHIBITS
4.1 Variables Entering the Study 45

TABLES
4.1 Psychometric Characteristics of the Dissent Toleration Scale (DISTOL 4D) 48
4.2 Hand-picked Items and Their Correlations With DISTOL 4D 58
4.3 Factor Analyzed Social Climate Items 59
5.1 Mean Values for Dissent Toleration—USA and FRG 67
5.2 Mean Scores for Independent and Conditioning Variables—USA and FRG 69

5.3	Zero-Order Correlations between School Social Climate Variables and Dissent Toleration—USA and FRG	70
5.4	Zero-Order Correlations between School Social Climate Variables and Civics Knowledge—USA and FRG	73
5.5	Correlation Matrix for Conditioning Variables, Social Climate (CLIME 1), Civics Knowledge, and Dissent Toleration—USA and FRG	75
5.6	Standardized Regression Coefficients (Betas) for Multiple Regression Analysis of Dissent Toleration and Civics Knowledge—USA and FRG	77
5.7	Standardized Regression Coefficients (Betas) for Multiple Regression Analysis of Dissent Toleration and Civics Knowledge using School Social Climate as a Contextual Variable—USA and FRG	81
5.8	Partial Regression Coefficients for Contextual and Non-Contextual Versions of Social Climate Scales	82
5.9	Standardized Regression Coefficients for the Regression of Social Climate Dimensions on Dissent Toleration and Civics Knowledge—USA and FRG	84
5.10	Dissent Toleration Regression Analysis by Type of Program—FRG	88

Acknowledgements

This study bears the imprint of many important influences in my academic and nonacademic life. First, Alex Inkeles provided me with an example of first rate cross-national research and introduced me to the study of learning environments. As my thesis adviser, he carefully monitored my progress and always provided prompt and insightful feedback. Hans Weiler introduced me to the study of dissent toleration and assisted in the development of the conceptual model for the study. His sound advice was also much appreciated.

In addition, I am indebted to the Spencer Foundation for financing my pre-doctoral year with the International Association for the Evaluation of Educational Achievement (IEA) in Stockholm, where I conducted the data analysis for this study. Torsten Husén, the Association chairman, was a most inspiring and generous host, as were my Swedish colleagues. While all were helpful and stimulating, Ingemar Fägerlind was particularly gracious in arranging institutional support and Mats Carlid most accommodating as a programmer and consultant. In addition, Spencer Foundation Fellow Edward ("Skip") Kifer generously and cheerfully shared with me his profound grasp of research methodology.

During the write-up phase of the research I benefited from the financial support of the Stanford Center for Research in International Studies. In addition, I have had the good fortune of working with Rudolf Moos of Stanford University's Social Ecology Laboratory, who provided many helpful suggestions and additional institutional support through NIMH Grant MH16026 and NIAAA Grant AA01863. I am also indebted to Judith Torney, senior author of the IEA Civics volume, who, under rather adverse conditions, carefully read my manuscript and provided valuable insights which guided its final revision. Of course, special words of thanks go to two exceptionally talented and gracious typists, Marily Thompson and Louise Doherty.

Finally, much praise goes to my parents, whose tangible and intangible supports sustained me through much schooling, and to my wife, Kay, who courageously submitted her desert-loving constitution to a long Swedish winter in order to be my helpmate.

Palo Alto, September, 1976

Abstract

This book probes into the relationship between the environment of schools and the learning of social conflict norms among approximately 4500 adolescents in the United States and the Federal Republic of Germany. The book stresses that knowing how to tolerate and cope with political dissent is just as important a socialization outcome as internalizing consensus or government support norms.

In both countries, school social climates which encourage independence of thought, emphasize concept (as opposed to rote) learning, minimize political ritual, and contain democratically run student peer groups, positively influence dissent toleration, both in a direct manner and indirectly by stimulating better understanding of democratic principles and institutions. The above relationship remained even when powerful conditioning variables such as social class background and verbal ability were controlled.

Differences between the countries were also noted, including the West German students' generally higher scores in dissent toleration, the more positive impact of student activism on political learning in the United States and the strong mediating position of ability grouping (tracking) between social class background and political learning in West Germany.

Some new methodological issues covered in the book were frameworks and methods for measuring learning environments in secondary data analysis, correcting for problems of perceptual tendency in environmental assessment by using classroom mean scores for individuals and the use of path analysis for testing a causal model for the development of dissent toleration.

Overall the analysis underscores the great importance that political learning, especially that concerning the theories and institutions of democratic government, has on the development of the norm of dissent toleration. Educators who are involved in this learning process should be aware of the learning climates they create, since the climate itself influences the rate and content of such learning. Systematic assessments of school and classroom environments can be carried out and the results fed back to teachers and students in order to assist them in creating more stimulating milieus for political learning.

Descriptors:
Civics, Political attitude, Tolerance, Socialization, International studies, School climate.

Chapter 1

Social Conflict and Dissent Toleration

> But nature knows better what is good for its kind; it wants discord.
>
> *Immanuel Kant*

Introduction

Politics in liberal democracies calls for constant balancing of consensus and conflict norms. Consensus is required in order to establish universalistic "rules of the game" which are prerequisites for social justice. Social conflict is inevitable as an expression of individual liberties and institutional change. In a democratic system consensus and conflict are linked together in a paradoxical way as illustrated by this statement by Smith and Lindeman (1951):

Persons striving to adapt themselves to the democratic way of life are required to discipline themselves to one variety of unity, namely unity which is achieved through the creative use of diversity. A society which is by affirmation democratic is expected to provide and protect a wide range of diversities. (p. 19)

Political socialization has typically been dominated by an interest in consensus norms. Connell and Goot (1972–73) have written a sharp indictment of political socialization research for its failure to focus on the inculcation of conflict norms. Weiler (1972) has emphasized the need for creative research into the nature, emergence, intensity and "successful" regulation of social conflict in order to redress the imbalance caused by the consensus bias in socialization studies. Such studies would not be conducted in order to replace "equilibrium theory" of sociology with a "conflict theory," but to develop a more dynamic, inclusive conception of society as a "tension management system." In the broadest sense, then, "a society encompasses conflict and its associated change as well as a social order that comprises tension-preventing and tension-managing devices and systems" (Inkeles, 1964, p. 27).

This study is a further attempt to redress the imbalance between conflict and consensus norms. As such, it draws upon the formulations of conflict theoreticians such as Coser (1956), Dahrendorf (1959) and Schattschneider (1960), as well as recent empirical studies by researchers like Weiler (1971), Grossman (1976) and Zellman and Sears (1971). The pages which follow will spell out more clearly the functions of political conflict, and the ways in which individuals might be socialized to cope with or manage conflict and dissent in the political arena.

The Role of Social Conflict in Democracies

In order to understand the role of social conflict, it is important that first the term be clearly defined. Simmel wrote that social conflict involves "a test of power between antagonistic parties" (Coser, 1956, p. 137). Elaborating on this theme, Coser (1956) indicates that status, power and resources are generally the values over which groups contend. Disagreement usually arises over the way in which such values are allocated by political authorities. Dahrendorf (1959) provides a basically non-Marxian approach to the analysis of social conflict, which goes beyond the dialecticians' claims concerning the historical necessity of interclass struggles. He asserts that every association of social groups involves two aggregates of authority positions, one of domination and the other of subjection. The first group is interested in the maintenance of the social structure, the other in its overthrow. Social conflict is the consequence. In his theory, social *classes* are involved to the extent that they represent the recruiting fields for the expression of group interests.

The above formulations concern the more diffuse aspects of conflict which pervade all facets of social relationships. In contrast, Schattschneider (1960) views social conflict from the particular perspective of a political scientist. His main assumption is that "the nature of political organization depends on the conflicts exploited in the political system, which is ultimately what politics is all about" (p. vii).

The socialization of conflict is a process by which the weak are able to bring their interests into the public arena in a way which counter-balances the power of the economically strong in private arenas. The exploitation of this situation is the essence of democracy: "the socialization of conflict is the essential democratic process" (p. 142).

All of the above authors have used the word "conflict" when referring to the relationships between antagonistic groups. Yet there are various degrees of conflict as well as many ways of expressing it. Some kinds of conflict involve the clash of ideas and ideologies, some involve the destruction of property and human beings, while still others involve the disregard or overthrow of social and cultural conventions. The first kind may be referred to as dissent; the second as violence, revolution or warfare; and the third as nonconformity. Much has been written about all three of these kinds of expressions of conflict (Dahrendorf, 1959; Blumenthal, *et al.,* 1972; Gurr,

1970; Stouffer, 1955). Often they have been used synonymously. The main focus in this study is with the clash of ideas and ideologies, that is, political dissent. Yet even within this subdivision there are many kinds of expression. Dissent may involve criticism of government policies or particular office holders or the system in general; it may involve acts of petitioning or protesting, the use of the written word, the spoken word or more symbolic acts, such as civil disobedience.

All of these forms of dissent play an important role in the functioning of a democracy. Besides being a way to bring private grievances to the public arena, dissent has four essential functions in a democracy. First, it serves to reduce error and ignorance; second, it contributes to the development of political freedom through "democratic restraint;" third, it increases government effectiveness by raising real issues; and fourth, it acts as a stimulus to social change.

The assertion that the flourishing of dissent and conflict reduces error and ignorance is one of the critical arguments of the great utilitarian thinker John Stewart Mill (1921). His words concerning the "open market place of ideas" are worth quoting:

Not the violent conflict between parts of the truth, but the quiet suppression of half of it, is the formidable evil: there is always hope when people are forced to listen to both sides; it is when they attend only to one that errors harden into prejudices, and truth itself ceases to have the effect of truth, by being exaggerated into falsehood. (p. 71)

These words were echoed in Twentieth Century America in the famous Supreme Court opinion of Justice Oliver Wendall Holmes (1010), as follows:

But when men have realized that time has upset many fighting faiths, they may come to believe even more than they believe the very foundations of their own conduct that the ultimate good desired is better reached by free trade in ideas—that the best test of truth is the power of the thought to get itself accepted in the competition of the market.

The concept of "democratic restraint" is presented in the study of political extremism by Lipset and Raab (1970). In a pluralistic society, restraint needs to be practiced by both government and citizens. In the first instance, individuals must be protected against the arbitrary use of power by those in authority. This can only be when citizens have the right to protest a government decision. In the second instance, citizens must be protected from intolerant behavior of other citizens. This means that each citizen must learn to restrain himself from the impulse to block another's freedom of expression. This is one of the most challenging aspects of democracy, for as Lane (1962) indicates:

Democracy asks men to support the rights of others to be heterodox, to say things that violate their moral and political codes, but they are brought up to believe in propriety and convention as a civilizing process. It is little wonder that democracy is a late product of history, and a painful achievement for some individuals. (p. 40)

The relationship of conflict to government effectiveness is highlighted by the following passage by Weissberg (1974):

If political action is to be more than ritualistic play-acting during which nothing ever happens despite enormous noise and commotion, significant divisive conflict must be present. Unless everyone agrees on everything—an obviously rare occurrence—conflict suppression or avoidance undoubtedly means that political choises are inconsequential ones between tweedledee and twedledum alternatives. Besides eliminating meaningful choices, conflict avoidance is an excellent means for suppressing demands for radical change. Where an unwillingness to face divisive conflict prevails, anyone seeking major changes is quickly labelled a troublemaker or out to rock the boat and therefore is readily dismissed with little serious attention to his substantive demands. Alternatives thus become nonissues, not through rational consideration, but rather through a psychological unwillingness or inability to face conflict-laden situations. (p. 69)

Finally, political dissent provides a stimulus to social change and facilitates organizational adjustment to changed conditions. This position is best defended by Coser and Dahrendorf. Coser (1956) emphasizes the function of conflict in creating new norms for changing social conditions:

Conflict acts as a stimulus for establishing new rules, norms and institutions... Furthermore, conflict reaffirms dormant norms and thus intensifies participation in social life... As a stimulus for the creation of norms, conflict makes the readjustment of relationships to changed conditions possible. (p. 128)

Dahrendorf (1967) stresses the importance of social conflict in increasing man's control over the rhythm of history:

Conflicts determine the speed, depth and direction of change. Whoever domesticates conflict by recognizing and regulating it may thus hope to control the rhythm of history. Whoever scorns such domestication has this rhythm as his enemy. Wherever conflicts are suppressed as awkward obstacles to arbitrary rule, or declared abolished once and for all, these falacies produce unexpected and uncontrollable responses of the suppressed forces. (p. 140)

Coping with Social Conflict

Social conflict in the political arena often poses a threat to governments and individuals. Those who would preserve the status quo have no use for conflict. Even promoters of social change sometimes fear that too much conflict will have undesirable effects. Thus there is a need to "domesticate" conflict. Once again Coser (1956) provides the key: "Conflict tends to be dysfunctional for a social structure in which there is no or insufficient toleration and institutionalization of conflict" (p. 157). Thus domestication of conflict requires both its institutionalization and its toleration. The problem of institutionalization includes at least three distinct aspects. First is what Schattschneider (1960) calls the "socialization of conflict." This unique usage of the expression "socialization" signifies a shift of conflicts from the private to the public arena. When conflicts are socialized, courts will settle disputes and political parties will articulate conflicting interests. In addition, in order for these processes to work, the "rules of the game" have to be such that neither of the conflicting parties is at a prestructured advantage or disadvantage.

Second, institutionalization involves the idea of legitimacy. Dahrendorf (1959) points out that the intensity of conflict decreases when the conflict groups are permitted to organize themselves and when "their issues become recognized." Lipset and Raab (1970) indicate that extremism and repression result when cleavage and ambivalence are treated as *illegitimate*.

Third is the aspect of adaptability. Huntington (1968) lists this as one of the qualities of an institutionalized political system. By this expression, he means the capability of a system to absorb challenges and to adjust to changing conditions. This would include the capacity of a government to cope with the conflicts which arise when power shifts from one political party to another.

Toleration of conflict involves a socialization of a different variety. It is socialization in the social psychological sense, in which values and predispositions of individuals are at stake. Much has been written on the topics of tolerance and prejudice, particularly after World War II (Adorno, Frenkel-Brunswik, Levinson, and Sanford, 1950; Christie and Jahoda, 1964). Studies from the "authoritarian personality" school attempted to show how early childhood experiences with authority could create deep-seated personality traits such as rigidity, submissiveness, conventionalism, superstition and cynicism, which would manifest themselves politically as right wing extremism. Rockeach (1960), departing from a similar psychoanalytical model, agrees that early experiences contribute to the structuring of a rigid belief system. This is the genesis and meaning of the "closed" or dogmatic mind. Important for him is not the ideological content of the belief system, however, but its structure. Thus, dogmatism of the right (authoritarianism) is not different *structurally* from dogmatism of the left. The open mind, on the other hand, is the mind which has structural flexibility. Such flexibility would allow one to tolerate ambiguity and diversity and would be more open to dissent and conflict.

Stouffer's *Communism, Conformity and Civil Liberties* (1955) offered further explanations for the existence of political intolerance in America.

His analysis of national survey data showed that tolerance was related to age, education and elite status. Mediating between these variables and tolerance were certain psychological constructs including: rigidity of categorization, authoritarian and conformist attitudes in child rearing, and optimism. Once again, psychoanalytical principles and early childhood experiences are involved in the explanation of intolerance, though it is apparent in Stouffer that later experiences, especially those found in school, also have important impacts.

More recent investigations have essentially abandoned the search for the roots of intolerance in early childhood experiences and basic personality traits. For example, in Lipset and Raab (1970) one finds an emphasis on the cognitive aspects of intolerance. People act to suppress certain groups often because they are insufficiently informed about the groups or because they have not fully understood democratic principles. Those who are more tolerant and are able to exercise democratic restraint, the "talented tenth," as Converse (1964) calls them, have formulated a comprehensive, well integrated political belief system. The others, the less tolerant, appear to lack a knowledge of "what goes with what." Important in Lipset and Raab's work is the distinction which they draw between "common democratic commitment" which involves affective attachment to a vague notion of civil liberties and "ideological democratic commitment" which involves a more uncommon attachment of both an affective *and* cognitive nature to democratic pluralism. It is "ideological democratic commitment" which allows for the full flourishing of dissent and conflict. The work by McClosky and his associates (1960, 1964) has shown that such a commitment is generally only found among the "articulate" classes. Their findings confirm those of Prothro and Grigg (1960), who contend that only an elite group (the "carriers of the creed") are capable of extending their beliefs in minority rights to concrete situations. Along the same lines, Selznick and Steinberg (1969) have demonstrated how intolerance of cultural diversity is related to a "primitive cognitive style" arising from the "common culture."

Summarizing the above, it seems clear that societies can "cope" with dissent through two main processes: the institutionalization of conflict and the socialization of tolerance. Up to this point, these two processes have been treated as if they acted independently. This, however, is certainly not the case in reality. The amount of conflict that a society or a particular individual can tolerate depends in part upon the level of institutionalization present in the political system. On the other hand, the degree to which conflict and dissent are institutionalized depends in part upon the amount of conflict people are willing to tolerate. Looking at the interrelationship from another point of view, some nations show a high degree of correspondence between the amount of conflict they can tolerate and the availability of institutions to channel such conflict. Other societies do not exhibit such congruence between their political culture and their political structure (see Almond and Verba, 1963, pp. 20—35). Thus, one cannot speak of the development of dissent toleration without some awareness that certain structural conditions are necessary before dissent and conflict can exercise their positive functions. Simon Schwartzman (1969), a Brazilian social scientist, makes this point when he states:

Only a "reasonable" level of conflicts—one sufficiently strong to stimulate change and adaptation on the part of political institutions but sufficiently weak to avoid situations of polarization, rigidity and loss of autonomy—could facilitate institutional development... The "optimal level of conflict" depends on previous contextual factors. (pp. 27—29)

Any comparative study of dissent toleration in two or more national contexts should thus consider the level of institutionalization of the countries involved. Failure to control for institutionalization could introduce considerable confusion into the interpretation of results, since differences in dissent toleration could reflect more about systemic capabilities (the existence of channelling institutions) than about individual values.

The Socialization of Dissent Toleration

In the literature on dissent toleration socialization reviewed above, two main theoretical approaches were identified. One approach placed a heavy emphasis on experiences (mostly, but not necessarily, of early childhood) which influence the *affective* domain of what has been termed the "personal system" (Inkeles and Levinson, 1963). The other, coming from a less psychoanalytic perspective, stressed the importance of development in the *cognitive* domain of the personal system. Using the model developed by Inkeles and Levinson (1963) for conceptualizing the personal system, the first approach could be said to be concerned with one's "personality structure;" the second with his "idea system." According to Inkeles and Levinson, attributes of personality structure include "character traits, core values, and moral standards, unconscious motives... and the like," which "play an important part in the internal functioning of personality and find manifold expression in a variety of life situations" (p. 222). Included in the personality structure could be "dogmatism," a variable which Stouffer, Rokeach and others have found to be an important determinant of dissent toleration. Included in the "idea system" are the various levels and kinds of "factual information, technical knowledge and empirical knowledge as culturally defined and validated" (p. 221). This system would include the facts and norms which are associated with democratic ideology as defined by Lipset and Raab (1970). It may also include some degree of commitment to such an ideology, although commitment is also partly an aspect of personality structure.

In sum, dissent toleration is a politically relevant value orientation which is influenced both by the individual's personality structure and his idea system. It is possible to refine this simple model a step further by identifying specific aspects within these constructs which are particularly relevant to dissent toleration. An important aspect within the personality construct is "dogmatism," or the extent to which one's responses to social stimuli are rigid and inflexible. Important within the construct of the idea system are "political cognitions," that is, the amount of information one has accumulated regarding political processes, principles and personalities.

Such aspects of the personal system are hypothesized to act as mediators between various social influences (socializing agents) and dissent toleration, as illustrated by Figure 1.1. In other words, a socializing agent influences dissent toleration by having an impact on both dogmatism and political cognitions. The model depicted in Figure 1.1 also indicates that under some circumstances the socializing agent can influence dissent toleration directly. It also shows that dogmatism and political cognitions can influence one another.

The top stream in the model, that leading through dogmatism, has already been investigated by Grossman (1976). Although in his study the linkage between the socializing agent (school environment) and dogmatism is ambiguous, the linkage between dogmatism and dissent toleration is clear: "respondents who have relatively more open belief systems tend to be more tolerant of dissent" (Grossman, 1976, p. 39).

The present study completes the model by concentrating on the lower stream of the model, that is, the effects of a school socializing agent on political cognitions and the effects of political cognitions on dissent toleration. There is one other linkage in the model of interest in this study: the direct link between the socializing agent and dissent toleration. Of course, as it stands, the model is greatly oversimplified. Many additional lines of influence will be added when the model is more fully specified in Chapter 2. The balance of this chapter will provide some background for the study of dissent toleration in the United States and the Federal Republic of Germany.

Dissent Toleration in the United States

In the United States, the ideal of unity in diversity (*E Pluribus Unum*) has been at the roots of the country's pluralist philosophy. Nevertheless, observers, including such men as Alexis de Tocqueville (1945), have sensed

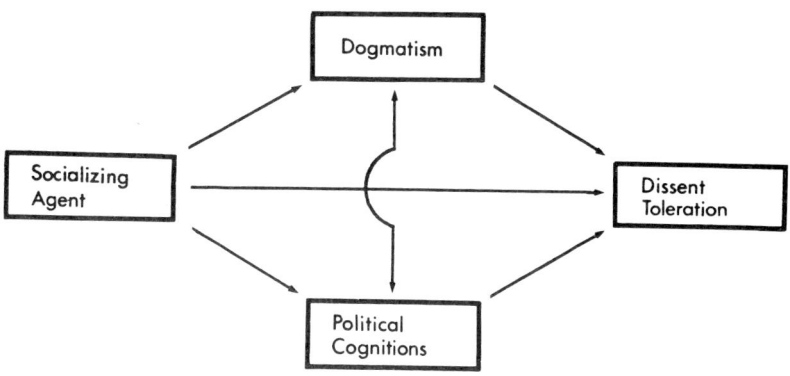

Figure 1.1. The General Socialization Model.

a tendency in American politics for an emphasis on unity at the expense of diversity. Indeed, there are indications that statesmen of the stature of Webster, Rush and Jefferson saw conformity as the price Americans must pay for liberty (Tyack, 1966). Such men, though in many other ways liberal and open to diversity, were fearful that the fragile ideals of the American Revolution would be undermined by less democratic European ideologies.

According to David Tyack (1966), Jefferson and his contemporaries meant to perpetuate ideological conformity through education. Schools were to be the agencies which would socialize the American way of life. There would be no room in the school for discussions of conflict and disorder in American history, especially of a kind which implied class, ethnic or racial antagonisms.

Contemporary research into political learning in American schools has revealed the extent to which a bias towards the socialization of consensus norms has been perpetuated. Remmers and his colleagues in the Purdue Opinion Panel (1963) discovered that a significant proportion of American high school seniors tested in the early 1960's did not endorse the freedom guaranteed by the United States' Bill of Rights. Hess and Torney (1967), through their surveys of political learning in elementary schools in the United States, have shown the relative absence of conflict themes in the political orientations of American children. A content analysis of school textbooks by Fox (1972) has shown the relative underrepresentation of conflict themes. And studies of teacher attitudes by Zeigler and Peak (1970) have revealed the generally conservative orientation of the typical American faculty. In summary, Weissberg (1974) indicates the status of conflict norms among American youth:

Despite the obvious necessity of some toleration of conflict in order for meaningful (rather than play-acting) political participation to occur, most American children fail to develop this orientation. Little doubt exists that Americans are overwhelmingly trained to prefer harmony and consensus to conflict. For example, many children show a genuine interest in elections and campaigns, yet nevertheless view any conflict between candidates as injurious to the nation. Even as children become politically more sophisticated, this aversion to conflict remains essentially unchanged. Children are deeply committed to the desirability of electoral contests, but the differences between the contestants—and hence the election's significance—must be kept to a minimum. (p. 69)

Dissent Toleration in the Federal Republic of Germany

The pluralist philosophy which was at the roots of American democracy appears never to have been part of German political tradition. According to Dahrendorf (1967), "There is a conception of liberty that holds that man can be free only where an experimental attitude to knowledge, the competition of social forces and liberal political institutions are combined. This conception has never really gained a hold in Germany" (p. 16).

Whether in the Imperial period, the Nazi period or even the modern-day period, the tendency in German politics has been to seek "authoritative and substantive rather than tentative and formal solutions." The tendency to seek ultimate solutions to social problems has fostered a general distaste for political solutions in Germany, particularly those which require arbitration between conflicting interest groups. The result in history has been a vicious cycle of conflict repression and radical change. It is Dahrendorf's (1967) conclusion that "the erratic changes of political systems in German history of the last hundred years may be described as a consequence of a fallacious attitude toward conflict in politics, as in the other institutional orders of society" (p. 140).

According to Dahrendorf (1967), this attitude towards conflict has been perpetuated partly because public values have never gained predominance over private values in Germany. In other words, public agencies, like the school, have never had more than a subsidiary role to the family in educating children. Kob (1963) found that parents and teachers concurred that the school should have a minimal influence on the attitudes of contemporary youth. Thus, even if the school were interested in fostering such public values as dissent and conflict toleration, it appears from the Kob study that its influence would be marginal.

A description by educational authorities of civic education in West German schools indicated that the country's schools placed a relatively low priority on teaching dissent and conflict toleration. The following concluding statement taken from the report of the West German Civic Education Committee (1967) indicates the extent to which training in conflict norms has been lacking in West German schools:

Taken as a whole, civic education in Germany has up to now (1967) presented an over-harmonious picture of the problems of state and society and developed a model of democratic society which is far too peaceful and free from conflict.

In civic education teaching in Germany, practical political thinking and a purified national conscience, which are the foundations of the political functioning of a democratic society, are scarcely touched upon. And yet on the other hand there prevails a belief, contrary to science, in the realisation of a conflict-free society, in which assertion of power is regarded as evil and the existence of conflicts is sinful. For this reason, power and strife, in spite of their being eminent political categories, and the conflict of powers and the great ideologists and foreign policy occupy only a very unsatisfactory position in the curricula for civic education in Germany.

Summary

Political conflict is as important for the functioning of a democratic form of government as political consensus. Nevertheless, in two large industrialized countries, the United States and the Federal Republic of Germany, political consensus has been stressed at the expense of political conflict. Traditionally in the United States, public socializing agencies functioned to promote conformity to the "American way of life." This way of life embraced civil libertarian values in the abstract, but in practice was suspicious of nonconformist and "alien" ideas. In the Federal Republic of Germany, a traditional preference for ultimate and objective solutions has undermined the development of an open and healthy attitude towards political dissent. Surveys conducted in both the United States and West Germany in the 1960's substantiate the claim that conflict norms received relatively little attention in the socializing agencies in the countries.

The purpose of this study was to assess the extent to which youth in the early 1970's in the two countries had internalized principles of dissent toleration and to determine the extent to which the school was involved in the socialization of open attitudes towards political conflict.

Chapter 2
Formal Education and Dissent Toleration

> The social climate in which a child lives is for the child as important as the air it breathes.
>
> Kurt Lewin,
> *Resolving Social Conflicts,* 1948

Introduction

Obviously, a personal orientation such as dissent toleration is influenced by a variety of social contexts including, besides the school, one's family, one's peers, voluntary social organizations, places of employment, and direct political experience. However, except for some places of employment and some voluntary associations, the school is the only setting of the above which is subject to direct public control in Western democracies. As such, the quality of the influence it exerts upon subjects is manipulable by means of public policy. Furthermore, in most countries the school is the public agency which occupies the greatest amount of a youth's available time. In fact, next to the family, the school occupies more of a youth's time than any other agency, public or private. Finally, the school has been shown to have powerful impacts upon political attitudes of youth (Hess and Torney, 1967; Langton, 1969; Dawson and Prewitt, 1969).

Within the school itself there is a great variety of aspects and influences which may impinge upon one's political orientations. Most commonly studied have been curriculum (Litt, 1963; Langton and Jennings, 1968; Prewitt, 1970; Azrael, 1965; Patrick, 1967; Fox, 1972; Jennings and Niemi, 1974) and teacher behavior (Zeigler and Peak, 1970; Christensen, 1960; Cogan, 1958; Biddle and Ellena, 1964). Less studied, but perhaps even more influential than the above, has been the impact of different learning environments. To conceive of a learning environment, one must conceive of schools as sociocultural systems, having characteristic sanctions, pressures, traditions, patterns of social interaction; organizational schemes, rhythms of work and the like (see Inkeles and Levinson, 1963). A more comprehensive view of the learning environment of schools is presented in Nielsen and Kirk, "Learning Environments and Learning Outcomes" (1973). For the purposes of this research, selected aspects of the learning environment found to be relevant and measurable in a variety of national settings will be used. Like dissent toleration, this variable is suitable for comparative research, for while it is difficult to compare the value of different curricula across cultures, it is somewhat easier to assess the nature of the environments in which the curriculum is presented.

The Impact of Formal Education

The studies dealing with tolerance mentioned in Chapter 1 appear to have one thing in common: they all reveal the preeminence of formal education as a predictor of tolerant attitudes. The studies by Stouffer, Selznick and Steinberg, Prothro and Grigg, and Lipset and Raab all show more educated adults to be significantly more tolerant than less educated adults. Related studies also show the powerful impact of education on politically relevant attitudes. The findings of Christie and Jahoda (1964) show the correlation between education and authoritarianism to be -.54. In their six country study, Inkeles and Smith (1974) show a median correlation of .20 between education and "minority opinion valuation." None of the above studies, however, has been able to demonstrate conclusively what it is about schooling that causes people who have more of it to be more tolerant of dissent. Indeed, some authors are beginning to doubt whether the advantages granted by more education are actually a result of "schooling" at all (Meyer, 1970).

Nevertheless, a scattered pattern of research and speculation has begun to give some shape to the relationship between education and dissent toleration. Lipset and Raab's (1970) research led them to conclude that for the development of democratic restraint, "the *kind* of education is... itself a powerful factor." Commenting on his findings that education was significantly related to tolerance of nonconformity, Stouffer (1955) speculates as follows: "What we will see [in our charts]... may be the effect, above all others, of a changing climate of education in both school and family." Weiler (1971) expresses the anticipation that further analysis will reveal the importance of "different institutional settings and their formal and informal characteristics" in the process of socializing dissent toleration. This speculative interest in the "kind", "climate", and "institutional setting" of education has set the stage for the present investigation of the effects of the social climate of schooling.

School Social Climates and Dissent Toleration

Most research on the effects of school social climates has been done fairly recently. (For a review, see Nielsen and Kirk, 1973, 1974.) Two different approaches have been taken to research in this area. First is the approach which conceives of the school social climate as a mediator of learning which is manifestly political in content. The other approach sees school climates as having an impact upon a child's development along lines which are indirectly related to politics in areas of latent political content. With regard to the first approach, there are those who, like Patrick (1967), believe that "political education programs would have a greater influence upon the formation of 'democratic' attitudes if they were conducted in an atmosphere more conducive to inquiry and open-mindedness." Ehman (1969) operationalized this concern for the atmosphere of learning in an important piece of research in which an "intellectually open" classroom climate became the link between the discussion of controversial issues and political efficacy, participation and cynicism. Langton (1969) used the related concept "degree of politicization" of the classroom as the mediator between school content and political efficacy. More germane to the interest of the present inquiry is Weiler's (1971) research in Germany which established a significant positive relationship between "discussion of controversial issues" and toleration of dissent among middle school students.

Also related to these concerns is the research of Walberg and Anderson (1968, 1972). They have found learning environments to be effective mediators of achievement in a variety of subject areas including math, physics, chemistry, biology, English, history and French. In a paper entitled "Social Environment as a Mediator of Classroom Learning," Walberg (1969) shows that "to encourage high rates of growth in achievement and understanding in classes, the social environment must be intellectually challenging." If this applies to the learning of physics, it should apply to the learning of civics as well.

The second approach to the impact of school climate is exemplified by Stouffer's (1955) study. In his view, the importance of the educational climate did not lie particularly in its function as a mediator of manifestly political messages, but in its capacity to motivate "the child to develop his own enthusiasms and incentives to learn." Important to Stouffer was the impact of the climate of education upon aspects of the personality such as rigidity of classification, authoritarianism, optimism and motivation.

Research by Almond and Verba (1963) also shows the effects of education on more general, politically latent variables. In their study, a school climate variable, the freedom to participate in school decisions, was measured as adults viewed it in retrospect and then related to a person's sense of subjective political competence. An underlying assumption in this analysis is that certain kinds of experiences create in students certain psychological predispositions, e.g., a sense of personal efficacy, which can later be transferred or generalized into the realm of politics. Such assumptions have been more fully elaborated by Dreeben in his book *On What Is*

Learned in School (1968). According to Dreeben, certain structural characteristics, such as the authority relationship between teacher and student, exert an influence upon the acquisition of particular social norms, including achievement, independence, universalism, and specificity. Once these norms have been socialized in one context, Dreeben maintains that they can be generalized to the political realm where they are essential to responsible citizenship. Along the same lines, such structural or organizational aspects of schooling could exert an impact upon the acquisition of norms for coping with political dissent. Once again, the principle of generalization would come into play: the way in which conflict is dealt with in class becomes a model for coping with conflict in the political realm.

The structural aspect of schooling of most interest to Dreeben was the social relationship between teacher and student. One of his principal goals was to show how this relationship differed in fundamental ways from the child's relationship with another type of authority figure, the parent. It is the encounter with this new kind of authority structure, one which is more impersonal and transient, that, in Dreeben's view, facilitates the development of the above norms.

Concern for the quality of the relationship between teacher and student did not, by any means, originate with Dreeben. An entire research tradition has developed around the problem of student-teacher relationships. Much of the research has been concerned with "leadership styles." Beginning with studies by Lewin, Lippitt, and White (1939), such research has investigated the differences between democratic and authoritarian leadership styles of teachers. Unfortunately, this tradition has failed to shed much light on the ways in which student-teacher relationships influence the socialization of democratic values. In fact, such studies have been devoted almost exclusively to assessing leadership effects upon achievement and morale. Moreover, findings in these areas have been shown to be of questionable validity. Anderson (1963) offers an explanation for this finding: "the authoritarian-democratic construct provides an inadequate conceptualization of leadership behavior." He continues with a prediction: "When a satisfactory body of knowledge about learning in social situations is available it will then be possible to describe the behaviors which a teacher can exhibit to achieve a given learning outcome."

More recent attempts to assess structural effects of schooling have moved away from the narrow concept of leadership styles and have begun to concentrate on the overall atmosphere or climate of the classroom. One conceptualization, that by Minuchin and her colleagues (1969), has used a battery of indicators to distinguish "traditional" school climates from "modern" ones. One of their findings has particular relevance to the model being developed in this study. They found that more modern school climates (i.e., more flexible, permissive, democratic, etc.) promoted more "differentiated and imaginative thinking in children." Such results occured not so much because the climate facilitated the learning of a different kind of curriculum, but because the social climate itself stimulated a different level of cognitive functioning.[1]

The above concept of "differentiated and imaginative thinking" is similar to certain other concepts which have been associated with toleration of dissent. I refer particularly to Stouffer's "enthusiasms and incentives to learn," and Zellman and Sears' "divergent thinking self-esteem," a concept which will receive more attention in the next section.

Another recent attempt to improve the conceptualization of structural effects of education is found in the work of Walberg (1969). This work has already been mentioned in connection with the mediating effects of learning environments. Some aspects of learning environments (e.g., difficulty) appear to mediate or predict learning outcomes, such as physics *achievement;* other aspects (satisfaction, friction, cliqueness) appear to be predictors of non-cognitive or special attitudinal outcomes, such as *interest* in physics. Walberg's Learning Environment Inventory (LEI) has also been used as a predictor of more diffuse social attitudes. Using a sample of elementary school children in Brazil, Holsinger (1972) found the learning environment to be a powerful predictor of attitudinal modernity. Though the LEI has not been used yet to predict dissent toleration, it is expected that a significant relationship could be found.

In summary, school and classroom climates are expected to influence dissent toleration in a variety of ways. If open and stimulating, they could enhance the acquisition of political knowledge. In such a process, social climate acts as a mediator of manifest political content. If, on the other hand, they encourage diversity and independence, they should exert a direct impact upon a student's personality structure, including the aspects of dogmatism and dissent toleration. The model elaborated in the first chapter is still relevant, but is now refined by another step. For "Socializing Agent", the expression "School Social Climate" is substituted. This is the expression I will use to aggregate all of the different aspects of school climate mentioned above. (See Figure 2.1 below.)

---

[1] This distinction is one made by Piaget. The acquistion of educational content or new information he calls learning. As shown above, this process can be mediated by the social climate of schooling. Another dimension to education is the growth of intelligence, which Piaget calls conceptual development. Social climates can have direct effects upon this dimension. (See Furth, 1970, pp. 72–74.)

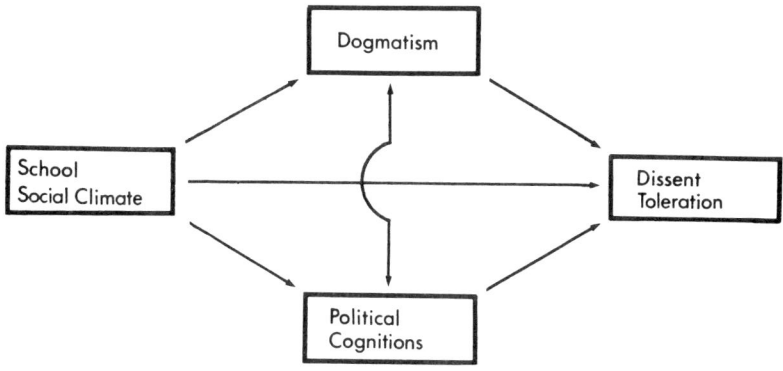

Figure 2.1. The Theoretical Model.

Political Cognitions and Dissent Toleration

In Chapter 1, the theoretical justification for placing political cognitions in the model as a predictor of dissent toleration was discussed. In brief, the theory is that those who *know* more about special groups and about democratic principles will be more likely to respond in a tolerant manner towards political dissenters. In the model elaborated in this study, this aspect of the idea system is conceived to be the construct of political cognitions.

Past research in this area has often attempted to measure this construct indirectly, by counting the number of civics courses a student had taken. Jennings, Langton and Niemi (1974, p. 198) showed that the number of civics courses taken had little effect on white students' "civics tolerance" scores. However, a moderate association was found between exposure and civics tolerance among black students. Remmers *et al.* (1963, pp. 56—57) found that completion of a high school course in civics or U.S. government was generally not related to a belief in the Bill of Rights. In fact, if anything, pupils who had completed such courses were less likely to endorse the Bill of Rights.

These findings are less disturbing when one realizes that completing a course does not necessarily mean learning anything. A more reliable measure of the effect of political learning on democratic values would employ some kind of achievement test to see actually how much a student had learned. This was done with some success in the research reported by Lipset and Raab (1970, pp. 505—510), which shows that the level of educational sophistication affects some aspects of democratic restraint.

The most comprehensive investigation ever in this area was that con-

29

ducted by the International Association for the Evaluation of Educational Achievement (IEA). In the summary Civic Education volume by Torney, Oppenheim and Farnen (1975), civics knowledge (as measured by an achievement test) was reported to be a significant predictor of anti-authoritarian values among 14-year-olds in eight countries. (The average proportion of the variance in anti-authoritarianism explained by civics knowledge was 5%.)

The current study uses the same IEA data base but examines a different dependent variable and explores the relationships in greater detail. Political cognitions are operationalized by using the same cognitive test mentioned in the preceding paragraph (Torney, Oppenheim and Farnen, 1975). In addition, several other sources of influence are controlled, according to the conceptual scheme to be outlined in the next section.

Conditioners of the Influence of Schooling

As a socializing influence, formal education does not act in a vacuum. Instead, it acts in a complex system in which its impact is moderated or conditioned by other socializing influences. Weiler (1973) has classified these influences or "intervening conditions" according to their temporal relationship to the schooling process. Thus, some conditions are *antecedent* to the schooling process, some are *concurrent* with it and some are *anticipated* during it. Since these conditioning variables are expected to be related both to the social climate variables and to dissent toleration, it is important to enter them into the analysis as controls so that challenges using alternative hypotheses can be met. By statistically controlling the effects of conditioning variables on the criterion, the independent effect of social climate can be more easily demonstrated.

Antecedent Conditions

The antecedent conditions which are most relevant to the model being developed in this study are student's sex, ethnicity, parental socioeconomic status, student's verbal ability and the type of educational program in which the student is enrolled. Stouffer's study (1955) showed women to be less tolerant than men. McDill and Rigsby (1973) found significant sex differences in explaining college aspirations and math achievement, girls being more influenced by "external attributes" (constraints of socializing agencies) than boys. Ethnicity has appeared as an important conditioning variable in several studies (Ehman, 1969; Jennings, Langton and Niemi, 1974). As was mentioned earlier, Jennings, Langton and Niemi (1974) found that the number of civics courses taken had more impact on civil tolerance among blacks than among whites.

Parental socioeconomic status is expected to condition the effects of schooling on both achievement and personality development outcomes. It is expected that children who come from higher status families where learning is encouraged and where verbal skills are more emphasized will be able to learn better. It is also expected that students from higher status families are less likely to have been exposed to rigid, authoritarian, intolerant parents (see Lipset, 1960, Chapter 4). A positive school climate could have a cumulative, reinforcing effect upon the values of those who are from higher status families. However, it might be argued that for them, such influences are redundant and that more positive school climates will have a greater effect upon those whose home climate is relatively closed (Langton and Jennings, 1968). In any case, it is expected that after controlling for social class background, schooling effects will still remain significant.

Student verbal aptitude is expected to be particularly important as a conditioner for civics knowledge. Those with higher aptitudes would be expected to learn faster and understand complex relationships better. It is not expected that I.Q. will explain all of the variance in civics knowledge, however. The climate of education is expected to show significant effects on learning outcomes even when aptitude is controlled (see Walberg and Anderson, 1972).

Finally among the antecedent variables is type of educational program. Most school systems have some kind of stratification according to student ability. Knowing the type of program a student is enrolled in (academic, vocational or technical) should indicate something about the character of the student's education. In all the IEA studies, including the one for Civic Education, this variable was used as a surrogate for past academic success (Peaker, 1975). Weiler (1971) used this variable as an anticipatory condition, maintaining that the completion of a particular course would result in the conferral of certain statuses in the future, the anticipation of which would cause the student to adopt particular status-appropriate attitudes. The power of the school to confer statuses through its particular "Charter" (Meyer, 1970) is part of a model which challenges the more traditional socialization model. The inclusion of type of program as a conditioning variable in this study is an attempt to control for both past academic success and the "Charter effect."

Concurrent Conditions

At the same time a youth is feeling the impact of schooling, he is also experiencing the influences of his family and other organizations. Home environment and religious activity are two concurrent conditions which are particularly relevant to the variables in my model. The importance of the home environments is underscored by the following statement by Moos (1973b):

... a classroom with a highly facilitative learning environment cannot have beneficial effects on student learning if the student lives in a family in which learning is devalued or ignored. Thus, the effects of school environments cannot be properly measured unless the other relevant community environments in which students function are also measured. (p. 20)

Of particular importance to dissent toleration is whether or not the student is granted some sense of independence from his parents. This could be measured by determining the extent to which a student's political and social attitudes are at odds with those of his parents. Having experienced conflict in the home, a youth may be better able to cope with conflict or even to expect it in other social contexts. Particularly if a student's parents are reasonable about conflict, a student may come to believe that he can disagree with members of his family without being suppressed or without destroying the structure of the family. This is clearly good training for being able to tolerate dissent in political life.

Besides the family, church organizations are often a significant part of the "community environment" of a student. There is some reason to anticipate that higher levels of religious activity will be negatively related to dissent toleration. Remmers *et al.* (1963) found that more "liberal" attitudes tended to be associated with lower intensity of religious belief. If a high level of religious activity is associated with a higher intensity of religious belief, and if intense religious belief is associated with dogmatism, then religious activity could be expected to predict low levels of dissent toleration. This proposition will be tested, since religious activity also enters the model as a conditioning variable.

Anticipatory Conditions

While in school, youth begin to formulate ideas about what they can expect in the future. Some youth anticipate relative affluence and upward mobility while others expect a life of economic hardship and few opportunities for changing their status. Some look forward to a college education after high school, while others are bound directly for the labor market. Some have clearly defined aspirations; others have only a vague notion of what they want. All of these alternatives are illustrative of different kinds of status expectations.

Such expectations about the future no doubt play a role in determining what is perceived and internalized in the present. For example, a number of recent studies (Langton and Jennings, 1968; Zellman and Sears, 1971; Weiler, 1971) have established the fact that college-bound youth are more tolerant of dissent than those not bound for college, even when social class background is controlled. It is asserted that those who are college-bound already have begun to adopt the values and attitudes of college-educated

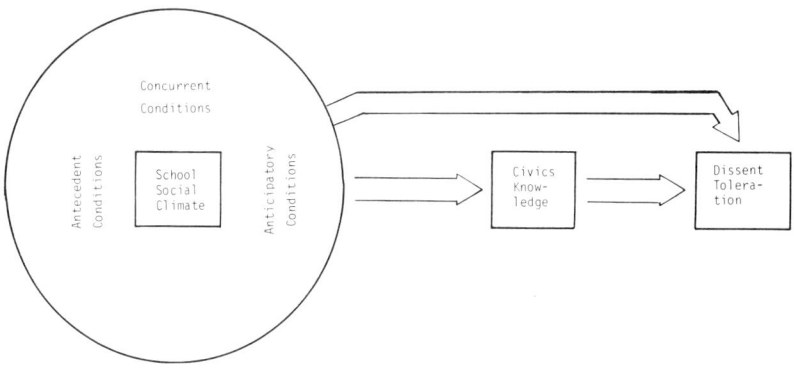

Figure 2.2. The Analytical Model.

adults ("anticipatory socialization"). College-educated adults are generally less authoritarian than the noncollege-educated (Lipset, 1960). The impact of expected education on dissent toleration could thus be an important anticipatory effect and is therefore also analyzed within the context of the model elaborated in this study.

The Analytical Model

Figure 2.1 summarized the basic structure of the theoretical model employed in this study. Since the stream through "dogmatism" will not be followed in this analysis, the analytical model will include only political cognitions as an intervening variable between school social climate and dissent toleration. The construct of political cognitions is measured by the IEA Civics Cognitive Test in this study. The Analytical Model in Figure 2.2 substitutes Civics Knowledge (the measured variable) for political cognitions (the concept) and places the conditioning variables in their places vis-a-vis the other main variables in the model.

Hypothesis Formulation

This chapter concludes by proposing the following hypotheses, based on the model elaborated in the previous section and the theoretical literature cited:
  After controlling for the conditioning variables,
  1) School Social Climate will have an independent, positive effect on Dissent Toleration, and

33

2) School Social Climate will have an indirect, positive effect on Dissent Toleration via Civics Knowledge;
which means that:
2a) School Social Climate will have an independent, positive effect on Civics Knowledge, and
2b) Civics Knowledge will have an independent, positive effect on Dissent Toleration.

Chapter 3

The IEA Data Set

IEA as a Research Enterprise

This study uses an extraordinary data set gathered by the national research organizations which participated in the International Association for the Evaluation of Educational Achievement (IEA). The research enterprise organized by IEA was unprecedented in the field of educational research for its scope and methodology. Twenty-one national research centers participated in some phase of a six-subject survey, which generated information about approximately 250,000 students, 50,000 teachers and 10,000 schools. Included in the survey are student achievement data in six subject areas: Science, Reading Comprehension, Literature, Civic Education and French and English as Foreign Languages. In addition to student achievement data, IEA gathered a substantial amount of information on students' homes, socioeconomic backgrounds, interests and attitudes. Furthermore, information was collected on backgrounds, attitudes and practices of teachers and on the characteristics of the schools.

From eight to 18 countries participated in each subject survey by testing students at one or more age levels: 10-year-olds (Population I); 14-year-olds (Population II); students in last year of pre-university schooling or programs of equivalent length (Population IV). Of the many countries which demonstrated interest in the Civic Education survey, ten finally participated in complete testing. In addition to the United States and the Federal Republic of Germany, this group of countries included Finland, Iran, Ireland, Israel, Italy, Netherlands, New Zealand, and Sweden. Table A.1 in the appendix lists the participating countries and the population levels at which they tested. Since the Iranian National Center requested that its data be withdrawn from cross-national comparisons, Iran does not appear in the table.

The IEA Civic Education Data

In one respect the Civic Education Survey is unique compared to the other subject area surveys. In the other five subjects cognitive achievement in the subject matter was the chief outcome of interest, while student attitudes were secondary concerns, used mainly as predictors of achievement. In the Civic Education study, attitudinal outcomes were placed at the same level of importance as cognitive outcomes in assessing the realms of Civic Education achievement. The decision was made based on the notion that Civic Education programs are established to convey not only the *facts* about national governments and international organizations but also the *values* and *attitudes* which are thought to be necessary and proper for active citizenship in a nation. In a sense, then, the IEA Civic Education survey developed into a large comparative study of political socialization.

The instrument construction phase of the Civic Education survey was, consequently, more sensitive and difficult than the corresponding phase in the other subject surveys. This phase was complicated by the fact that in Civic Education, in contrast to mathematics or science, there was no clear concept of the boundaries of the subject matter, especially when considered in an international perspective. Therefore, the directors of the participating national centers were obliged to meet together frequently to compare national curricula and supporting documents in order to define the subject area. Although there were rather wide-ranging variations in the kinds of courses considered to be Civic Education in different countries, the IEA countries were finally able to arrive at a set of themes which were considered common to the curricula of all participating countries. The following six themes were emphasized in all of the participating countries to one degree or another:

1. Understanding rights and obligations: respect for others, tolerance, loyalty, belief in equality, respect for law, willingness to defend the homeland
2. Support for the democratic way of life: belief in freedom of the individual, right of citizens to express dissent, right to be represented; willingness to participate by voting
3. Appreciation of world interdependence and amity
4. Respect for government and for national tradition without ethnocentrism
5. Respect for diversity in moral and religious values, as well as respect for political opposition
6. Interest in current events and social problems at national and international levels.

The fact that toleration of dissent is directly or indirectly mentioned in three of the six common themes was a strong indicator that these countries could be used in a research project concerned with the socialization of dissent toleration. A closer examination of the country curriculum statements shows that dissent themes are covered in both the United States and the Federal Republic of Germany, though they appear to be emphasized in the formal curriculum of the latter country more than in that of the former (see Torney, Oppenheim, and Farnen, 1975, Chapter 1).

Development of Research Instruments

Cognitive Instruments

The instruments for measuring cognitive and affective outcomes in Civics were created by separate international subcommittees. The cognitive achievement instruments were developed according to essentially the same procedures employed by the developers of previous IEA tests. That is, a large grid of themes was constructed which included items at different levels of difficulty. Each country was asked to indicate whether the items were covered in their country's schools and then instructed to submit items which could be used to test whether or not the items had been learned by students. Of the hundreds of questions submitted, the committee chose those considered most likely to be cross-nationally valid and grouped them into several versions of a questionnaire for each age level. These versions of the instruments were pretested in most of the participating countries, including the United States and the Federal Republic of Germany. On the basis of the pretests, items which were too easy or difficult or which did not discriminate well were eliminated. New versions of the instruments were then distributed to national centers and once again subjected to criticism by experts from the various countries. When the final versions of the questionnaires (one for each sampling population) were settled upon, they were used in a "Dry Run," which occurred in the spring of 1970.

The Civics Cognitive test used in the actual survey in Population II, the age group of interest in this thesis, contained 47 questions, each having one predetermined correct (or keyed) response. Four other alternatives were given as distractors. The test was scored by summing the number of correct responses and then correcting this raw score through the use of a guessing formula (see Choppin, 1974). A copy of the Civics Cognitive test for Population II is found in the Appendix, part B.

Attitudinal Instruments

Measuring political attitudes was considerably more difficult than measuring acquired civics knowledge. This was chiefly because the boundaries in the attitudinal domain were even less precisely drawn. The domain for civics knowledge was more or less clearly defined in the particular countries by curricular statements and school texts. The domain for political attitudes was also defined in printed curricular statements, but, in addition, included a vast array of content which was not part of the formal curriculum and not restricted to civic education programs. The problem was further complicated by the fact that political attitudes develop as often as *unintended* consequences of schooling as *intended* consequences. For example, one could conceive of a situation in which a formal school program encouraged the development of positive attitudes towards citizen participation, but the school's organizational structure discouraged student participation. An unintended consequence in this case might be low political efficacy. Thus, many important areas of political attitude content were not suggested by curricular statements and had to be gleaned from other sources, particularly the growing literature on political socialization.

An additional problem arose in adapting the interesting themes to the level of understanding of children and adolescents. Since many of the attitudinal themes of interest were either quite abstract or connected with behaviors (such as voting) which were far in the young person's future, rather extensive pretesting procedures had to be followed. Instead of using national experts as judges of appropriate test content, the committee in charge of developing the attitudinal instruments collected extensive information directly from the children, making use of projective and interactive techniques in pretests.

Two main domains of political attitudes were identified as a result of pilot interviews in several countries: democratic values and citizenship. A variety of instruments were then designed employing various measurement techniques, including projective questions, attitude statements, check lists and forced choice items. These instruments were pretested in several countries including the United States and the Federal Republic of Germany in 1968. Refinements of the instruments were made on the basis of factor analyses, intercorrelations, and item analyses. The same items were tried out at all population levels.

Since this analysis focuses mainly on items within the domain of "democratic values," only items which were used to measure this domain will be treated in detail here. The tests of "citizenship values" and a special instrument called "How Society Works" are discussed at length in Torney, Oppenheim and Farnen (1975) and in a monograph by Oppenheim and Torney (1974) called *The Measurement of Children's Civic Attitudes in Different Nations*.

In conceptualizing the domain of democratic values, the committee included the following dimensions or principles: equality, civil liberties, majority rule, women's rights, tolerance of diversity and racial equality. Items covering these dimensions were chosen and carefully translated (and in some cases back-translated). The statistical technique used to establish cross-national comparability was factor analysis. After the 1970 "dry run" in which all instruments were administered to judgment samples in seven countries, a factor analysis was conducted which revealed the same basic four-factor structure for the democratic value domain in all participating countries. According to Torney, Oppenheim and Farnen (1975), "Bearing in mind the generalized and highly complex issues in the political sphere, the fact that these attitudes are not yet stable or fully formed in children of this age group, the radically different composition of the item pools, the problems of translation and of cultural differences... the striking finding is the clarity and consistency of the results of these factor analyses" (pp. 174–175). The specific attitudinal items used in the present study will be given in Chapter 4.

Background Information

Since IEA represented such a large network of organizations and scholars, each with its own special interests and theories, the limitation of the amount of information to be collected presented a special problem. Of the many alternatives available for data collection strategies, IEA opted to collect a broad spectrum of information on large samples of students, leaving each country free to conduct more in-depth surveys as follow-up studies. Thus the background information collected for IEA research is a rather eclectic collection of factors which were thought by members of the various committees to influence educational achievement.

The broad design of IEA required that certain basic background variables be measured in each survey. These variables included student family background variables, a verbal ability measure, general student attitudes about school and information about a school's organization, funding, staffing and control (as reported by a school administrator). In addition each subject committee was encouraged to develop questionnaires which would yield information useful in predicting student achievement in the specific subject area. The particular set of background variables developed for the Civic Education Survey included a wide variety of factors ranging from the student's interest in public affairs television, through the student's perception of classroom climate and procedures, to the degree of student rejection of parental values. Most of these items were developed "from scratch" for the Civic Education Survey, though some, for example, the classroom climate scales, borrowed heavily from the work of previous researchers (e.g., Walberg and Anderson, 1968).

Sampling in the Two Countries

The decision to focus on students from the United States and the Federal Republic of Germany was based on a variety of factors. First was the matter of institutional context. As was mentioned in Chapter 1, the level of conflict a society as a whole can tolerate depends to a large extent upon the existence of institutional channels for the mediation of conflict. Having democratic forms of government, both the USA and the FRG have operative political parties, a variety of forums for public debate, including a relatively free press, and viable, authoritative court systems. Thus both countries were viewed as having political infrastructures sufficiently institutionalized to channel and cope with significant levels of dissent and conflict.[1]

In addition, the problem of political tolerance is a salient one among educators and social scientists in both countries. This is apparent from the content of formal curricular statements in the two countries and from the thrust of contemporary research, some of which was reviewed here in Chapter 1.

Another factor was the fact that, perhaps more than any other pair of IEA countries, the two were similar in their basic social and economic infrastructures. Both West Germany and the United States are highly developed industrialized countries having complex and bureaucratized institutions. In both countries the government structure is a federalized one, which means, among other things, that education policy is set by state and local law. Politically the two countries operate in the context of a small number of major national political parties (two in the USA; three in the FRG), and both have experienced changes in the controlling party in recent years. Economically the two countries also have similar profiles. Both have fewer than 10% of their labor force in agriculture and more than 70% of their populations living in urban areas. Finally both are relatively wealthy countries as evidenced by their high GNP's per capita which were US$4,440 for the USA in 1972 and US$2,520 in 1970 for the FRG. (See Chapter 3 of Torney, Oppenheim and Farnen, 1975.)

Educationally the two countries also have similar profiles, at least until the level of upper secondary and higher education. Compulsory education begins at age 6 in the United States and ends at age 16. In the Federal Republic of Germany the corresponding ages are 6 and 15. The modal age of transfer from primary to secondary school in the USA is 11—12 years; in the FRG, 10—12. The proportion of the 14-year-old age cohort, the age group of interest in this thesis, in school in the United States is 99%; in the Federal Republic it is 94%. After age 15 the education profiles of the two countries diverge considerably. For example, in 1969 the percent of university-aged students attending an institution of higher education in the United States was 40%; the comparable figure for the Federal Republic was 12%.[2]

One of the reasons for focusing this research on 14-year-olds is precisely

---

[1] This point could be debated in the case of the Federal Republic of Germany. In a recent book Sontheimer (1972) argues that there has been a change in the political life of the Federal Republic toward the "anchoring of the liberal democratic system." Yet he adds that this new consensus could break down somewhat in the face of severe economic or external pressures.

[2] Education profiles taken from Torney, Oppenheim and Farnen, 1975, Chapter 3.

because such a high proportion of the age group is enrolled in school in both countries. Another reason was that by this age youth are able to apply the kind of abstract reasoning necessary for the development of dissent toleration. Weissberg (1974) supports this notion when he writes, "A six-year-old cannot understand the concept of civil liberties (though he knows that freedom is a good thing), but by thirteen he has most likely formed an opinion on freedom of the press and toleration of dissent" (p. 29). Political orientations are certainly not immutably set by these early teenage years; much intellectual growth and experience will occur before an adolescent will be able to act as a full citizen. Yet, as Weissberg (1974) points out, "in certain broad issue areas individuals tend to operate within bounds set by earlier political socialization" (p. 29).[3]

Now that it is clear why two particular populations were singled out from the IEA Data Bank for this study, the sampling procedures followed by IEA will be described. Population II, the target population of this study, was strictly defined as all students aged 14 years and no months to 14 years and eleven months and in full-time schooling at the time of testing.

Since it was the aim of IEA research to make general statements about the student population, national probability samples were sought. Typically two-stage stratified probability sampling was employed. In the first stage, schools were selected from a nationally stratified frame with a probability proportional to the size of their student body (e.g., a school with 90 students would have three times the probability of being chosen than a school with 30 students). At the second stage, students were to be selected randomly from schools with a probability inversely proportional to the size of the school (e.g., if both the schools above were chosen, all of the students from the school with 30 students would be selected and 1/3 of the students from the school with 90 students would be selected). In this way, approximately the same numbers of students (30) were to be drawn from each school, with each student in the population having the same chance of entering the sample. Because of its size, the United States was obligated to add a prior sampling stage, community, to the other two stages. Thus in that country, communities were first randomly sampled, next schools and then students.

According to the rules established by IEA, the participating countries, including the two chosen for this research, were called upon to submit their specific plans for sampling to an International Sampling Referee. After appropriate amendments were made to these plans, they became known as the Design Sample. A National Technical Officer in each country directed the actual process of contacting and securing the cooperation of schools. As

---

[3] See also Richard E. Dawson and Kenneth Prewitt, *Political Socialization* (Boston: Little, Brown, 1969), p. 61.

expected, for various reasons the Executed Sample did not correspond exactly with the Design Sample. This was especially true in West Germany where the refusal rate of schools was exceptionally high. Even though a parallel sample was prepared in that country, still only 49 of the 148 designated schools took part in the survey. This shortfall is partly explained by the fact that one of the ten *Bundesländer*, Nordrhein-Westfalen, withdrew from the survey shortly before full field testing. Thus, strictly speaking, the sample for the Federal Republic of Germany falls short of being a national sample.

After examining and cleaning the data, it was found that an additional few schools had to be eliminated because of incomplete data. This cleaned student sample, known as the Achieved Sample, was the student sample used in the present study.

In addition to the student sample, the countries were to randomly select an average of 5 teachers per school from among those teaching the subject matter. In the Achieved Sample, the FRG was nearly able to meet that standard; the USA was only able to select an average of about 2.5 teachers per school. Practical considerations prevented IEA from matching teachers from a school with students from the same school. That fact, plus the fact that there were so few teachers represented (especially in the USA), resulted in generally low or zero correlations of the teacher variables with student variables. Thus only a few teacher variables entered the early stages of this study and none entered the final anslyses.[4]

In order to bring each country's Achieved Sample into correspondence with the Design Sample, weights were assigned to students according to whether their stratum had been over- or undersampled. In order to correct for under-sampling in a stratum, students were given weights greater than 1.00; to correct for over-sampling students were assigned weights smaller than 1.00. The weights for all students in a country average out to exactly 1.00, meaning that the sum of weights is equivalent (with slight rounding errors) to the number of students tested. Weighted student data will be used on all cases in this analysis except where otherwise indicated.

The Achieved Sample sizes for Population II students and teachers in the United States and the Federal Republic plus the average grade level of the students are as follows:

---

[4] The teacher variables were finally eliminated because they did not scale with the other independent variables. In a school level factor analysis, none of the teacher variables had loadings on a factor as high as student level variables.

	Schools	Teachers	Students	Average Student Grade Level
United States	129	317	3207	9.0
Federal Republic of Germany	48	218	1317	8.2

Collection and Treatment of the Data

After the instruments were put into their final forms and printed, and the samples drawn, the next step was the actual collection of the data. National Technical Officers directed the data collection in the two countries. They were assisted in each school by school coordinators, who were usually, but not always, the school principal or headmaster. All of the procedures followed by the National Technical Officers and school coordinators were outlined in detail in three instruction manuals. These spelled out sampling procedures and methods of distributing, collecting, and coding the paper and pencil tests and questionnaires. In most cases Machine Readable Cards (MRC) were used as answer forms to facilitate processing.

The school coordinators were directly responsible for filling out the school questionnaire and for administering the teacher questionnaires. They were also responsible for choosing and briefing test administrators (generally classroom teachers or university students).

Test administrators were given strict guidelines for administering tests and questionnaires. Tests were timed according to international time limits; questionnaires were to be given in a standardized sequence but not timed. Test administrators were instructed not to help students answer test or opinion questions, but were encouraged to assist students with factual questions on the background questionnaires. The average time for completing the battery of Civic Education materials was approximately two hours. After the testing was completed, all material was sent in a bundle to the National Centers.

National Centers had the responsibility of ensuring that the identification sections on all the forms were correctly filled in and of performing certain post-coding operations. When the data had all been punched on IBM cards, they were sent to a data processing center at Columbia University, New York, where student, teacher and school files were created. Corrected test scores were computed at this stage and certain scales were constructed. From New York these files were sent on tape to the IEA international headquarters in Stockholm, Sweden, where they were compiled into "merge files." In these files each student was assigned scores for items from the school questionnaire and scores for the average response of the teachers in his school to the teacher items. The student merge files for the United States and the Federal Republic of Germany provided the raw data for this study. Special variables and scales were constructed from these data by the author particularly for its analyses. Their creation and treatment will be discussed in the chapter which follows.

Summary

The empirical analysis performed in this study is based on data collected by the International Association for the Evaluation of Educational Achievement (IEA) for two countries, the United States and the Federal Republic of Germany. These countries are particularly suited for a comparative analysis because they have similar political, economic and educational profiles. The study focuses on 14-year-olds because they are the IEA population which is both highly representative of their age cohort and old enough to have developed ideas about abstract political topics.

Since the IEA Civic Education survey was an unprecedented cross-national research enterprise, most of the research instruments used were new and original, created by a unique international committee which relied heavily on national documents, the judgments of experts and the results of extensive pilot and pretesting efforts. A battery of standardized tests and questionnaires was eventually developed which measured civics cognitive achievement, political attitudes and various personal and family background factors.

Sampling was conducted according to an international sampling design supervised by a sampling referee. Stratified national samples were drawn according to plan and deviations were compensated for through the use of student weights. Since one of the German *länder* withdrew from testing in the Federal Republic of Germany, the sample from that country cannot be considered a strict national sample.

The data collected from over 4500 students in the two countries were checked and processed by an international data processing center and packaged into well-documented and highly serviceable student merge files at the IEA international headquarters in Stockholm. The raw data for the analysis which follows was drawn from the merge files for the United States and the Federal Republic of Germany.

Chapter 4
Measurement of the Variables

One of the first tasks in conducting the research was to reconcile the theoretical model elaborated in Chapter 2 with the data set available from the IEA survey. Since this study was conceived after the collection of the IEA data, it was not possible to directly influence the content and form of the raw data. Nevertheless, most of the concepts of theoretical interest were found to be operationalizable using the Civic Education data. Inevitably, there were some cases in which the data set did not allow for the ideal operationalization of a concept. Exhibit 4.1 presents a list of the variables which enter this study. This chapter discusses the ways in which these

Exhibit 4.1   Variables Entering the Analysis

Dependent Variable

Dissent Toleration

Independent Variable

Social Climate of Schooling

> Classroom Equality
> Peer Group Interaction
> Independence of Thought
> Academic Climate
> Political Environment
> Ritual Climate of Classrooms
> Teacher Control
> Student Power

Control or Conditioning Variables

Antecedent Conditions

> Student Sex
> Parental Socioeconomic Status
> Verbal Ability (Word Knowledge)
> Type of Educational Program

Concurrent Conditions

> Religious Activity
> Conflict with the Family

Anticipated Condition

> Educational Expectations

Intervening Variable

Civics Knowledge

variables are measured using IEA data. It will also indicate the extent to which compromises had to be made in the operationalization of a variable.

Operationalizing Dissent Toleration

Choosing Appropriate Indicators

The main purpose of this study is to show the extent to which a student's capacity to tolerate dissent is related to the kind of social climate he is exposed to at school. As such, dissent toleration is the main dependent variable of the study.

The concept of dissent toleration has not been widely used in political socialization research. Thus, there has not been a research tradition to draw upon for instrument construction. Weiler's study (1971) is pioneering in this regard. His measures of dissent toleration presented various kinds of nonconformist or deviate behaviors and asked the respondent to indicate how he would react socially to one who engaged in such behaviors. Such an operationalization is effective because it ties dissent toleration to concrete situations and because it provides a measure of the various latitudes of acceptance or rejection of dissenters and their behavior. Although this is a most effective way to measure dissent toleration within a nation, it becomes problematic when replication in a different nation is contemplated. Weiler's scale is tied to various controversial issues in West Germany's current affairs. In order to replicate this scale, one would have to find issues which were equally controversial in the new country. Obviously, there is no sure way of guaranteeing such equivalence.

Another approach would be to find a set of hypothetical situations for the expression of political dissent which occur in democracies everywhere. An example of such a situation is a group of people organizing to protest a government decision. Such a situation is general enough to have cross-national meaning, but not too general to become a platitude with which no serious person would disagree.

Fortunately, the IEA data set contained several items of this kind. A factor analysis performed by Oppenheim and Torney (1974) revealed the patterning of several of the same factors in all of the Civic Education countries, including the following three factors of special significance to this study:

1. Tolerance and support for civil liberties,
2. Belief in the value of criticism of government, and
3. Active perception of citizenship.

It is from these three factors that the items in the dissent toleration scale

are drawn. The following 13 items were selected because each one dealt with some aspect of political dissent:
1. Newspapers and magazines should be allowed to print anything they want except military secrets.
2. People should be allowed to come together whenever they like.
3. Citizens must always be free to criticize the government.
4. People who disagree with the government should be allowed to meet and hold public protests.
5. When something is wrong, it is better to complain to the authorities about it than to keep quiet.
6. It is good for a government to be frequently criticized.
7. The people in power know best. (reverse coding)
8. It is wrong to criticize our government. (reverse coding)
9. People should not criticize the government, it only interrupts the government's work. (reverse coding)
10. Colored people should have (more, exactly the same, fewer) rights and freedoms than (as) everyone else.
11. Communists should have (more, exactly the same, fewer) rights and freedoms than (as) everybody else.
12. People with anti- (insert name of mother nation) views should have (more, exactly the same, fewer) rights and freedoms than (as) everybody else.
13. A good citizen tries to change things in government.

The first nine items test the respondent's level of agreement with various statements about the value of criticism and protest with respect to the government. The next three items test the respondent's willingness to grant full rights and freedoms to minorities and nonconformists. The last item tests the respondent's feelings about good citizenship, i.e., whether one who tries to change things in government (a dissenter) is considered a good citizen. The exact wording of the questions is found in the Appendix, part C.

Constructing the Dissent Toleration Scale

Various combinations and codings of the above items were tried in order to maximize the validity, realiability and cross-national comparability of the scales. The first version of the scale, DISTOL 1, consisted of all 13 items, coded with the original questionnaire values. The next scale was DISTOL 1D, which dichotomized all of the items so that each was given equal weight in scaling. On the next wave, certain items which appeared to have little cross-national comparability were eliminated. In DISTOL 3D, for example, item 10, concerning "colored people", was eliminated, since the FRG does not have a most significant racial minority. In DISTOL 4D, both items 10 and 11 were eliminated. Item 11 was eliminated because the Communist Party has had different histories in the two countries and there was no way to guarantee that this organization was perceived as the same kind of threat to the status quo in each national context.

In the end, it was the eleven item scale, DISTOL 4D, which was chosen for this analysis. The reliabilities of the scale, computed according to the Kuder-Richardson formula for dichotomized scales (KR-20) are given in Table 4.1. The coefficients, .64 and .59, for the USA and the FRG are acceptably high, considering the number of items in the scale (11).

The validity of the scale could not be determined directly. Since it was developed after the data were collected, there was nothing built into the IEA survey which could clearly validate it. However, one indication of the scale's validity is how well it covaries with other measures thought to be related to dissent toleration. One such measure is the test of Civics Knowledge. The correlation between DISTOL 4D and Civics Knowledge was approximately .50 for both countries (.47, USA; .51, FRG). This is, of course, one of the main outcomes of interest in the study. At the same time, however, it gives some assurance that the Dissent Toleration is an adequately valid measure. Looking across all eight countries of the IEA survey, the scale correlates with the more objective civics test at an average of .45. This was interpreted as sufficient evidence of its cross-national validity.

Table 4.1 also lists the item-to-scale correlations for DISTOL 4D in both countries. The pattern of correlations for the first nine items is remarkably similar for the two countries.

Table 4.1   Psychometric Characteristics of the Dissent Toleration Scale (DISTOL 4D)

a. Item to Scale Correlations

Item		USA	FRG
1.	Newspapers and magazines should be allowed to print anything	.36	.38
2.	People should be allowed to come together whenever they like	.37	.37
3.	Citizens must always be free to criticize the government	.59	.51
4.	People who disagree should be free to protest	.53	.51
5.	When something is wrong, it is better to complain	.43	.40
6.	It is good for the government to be frequently criticized	.50	.57
7.	The people in power know best (reverse coding)	.36	.38
8.	It is wrong to criticize our government (reverse coding)	.65	.66
9.	People shouldn't criticize government; it interrupts work	.54	.63
12.	People with anti-national views should have the same rights	.35	.27
13.	A good citizen tries to change things in government	.33	.17
b. Kuder-Richardson (20) reliability		.64	.59

The most highly correlated items are the five which deal with criticism and protests in both countries. The other four items, though less strongly correlated with the overall scale than the first five, have virtually the same coefficients in the two countries.

The last two items in the scale, the one concerning the rights of "antinationals" and the one concerning the behavior of a good citizen, are somewhat different in their relationships to the total scale in the two countries. In short, they are both more strongly correlated with the scale in the United States than in the Federal Republic.

The item-to-scale correlation of the last item, the one regarding good citizenship, is considerably stronger in the United States than in the Federal Republic. This seems to indicate that in the United States (more than in West Germany) dissent is not just tolerated but seen as part of good citizenship. It probably also reflects the generally higher level of support for participant citizenship in the United States—a phenomenon which has been well documented in the literature (Almond and Verba, 1963; Sontheimer, 1972; Torney, Oppenheim and Farnen, 1975).

Following the IEA pattern of analysis, identical scales were used in the two countries to represent the criterion variable, i.e., the same 11 items in both countries. This approach meant that the reliability of the West German scale was suppressed somewhat compared to that of the United States, as has been demonstrated. Since there were generally higher correlations between this scale and predictor variables in the Federal Republic than in the United States, the decision did not seem to have detrimental effects on the analysis in that country.

In summary, the concept of dissent toleration was operationalized by using the IEA Civics survey items which presented hypothetical situations or dissenting groups and measured the students' reactions to them. A scale, DISTOL 4D, was developed which had acceptable levels of reliability and validity for the two countries and which was cross-nationally comparable.

Operationalizing School Social Climate

Dimensions of Social Climate

The independent variable, social climate of schooling, has, like dissent toleration, only recently been of interest to researchers. Thus there are no standard definitions or usages of the concept in the education research literature. Reviews of the school climate literature (Nielsen and Kirk, 1973, 1974) showed "social climate" to be just one dimension of the "sociocultural system" within the school. In an innovative paper, Inkeles and Levinson (1963) proposed that the socio-cultural system of an organization could be studied in much the same way as the personal system of an individual. In their proposed framework for analysis, four sets of organization properties, each analogous to a personal property, are elaborated: 1) ecological properties; 2) cultural properties; 3) structural properties; and 4) social process characteristics.

Moos (1973b) carries the isomorphism between personal attributes and organizational properties even further. He writes:

> The social climate perspective assumes that environments have unique "personalities." Methods have been developed to describe a person's personality. Environments can be similarly portrayed with a great deal of accuracy and detail. For example, some people are supportive; likewise, some environments are supportive. Some men feel the need to control others; similarly, some environments are extremely controlling. Order and structure are important to many people; correspondingly, many environments emphasize regularity, system and order. People make detailed plans which regulate and direct their behavior; likewise, environments have overall programs which regulate and direct the behavior of the people within them. (p. 8)

Moos' analytical framework, similar in many ways to that of Inkeles and Levinson, isolates six dimensions of human environment which have been of interest to scholars: 1) ecological dimensions; 2) behavioral settings; 3) dimensions of organizational structure; 4) dimensions identifying the collective personal and/or behavioral characteristics of the people living and functioning in the environment; 5) variables relevant to the functional or reinforcement analyses of environments; and 6) dimensions which assess social and organizational climates.

A truly comprehensive scheme for assessing the impact of school environments on the individual would include all of the above dimensions. Yet for several reasons, this was found to be an impossible task for the present study. First of all, the study is limited by the types of measures used by IEA, and these measures did not cover all of the above dimensions. Second, the study is limited by theoretical considerations. Since a specific attitudinal outcome, dissent toleration, is the main object of analysis, the environment dimensions can justifiably be limited to those judged to be most relevant to the fostering of this outcome. In connection with this idea, Gillespie and Ehman (1974), who have themselves attempted to map out the politically relevant dimensions of social environments, have stated: "It is only through such a framework that we can begin to see how school environments in their full dimensionality affect students' political attitudes and behaviors" (p. 4).

Of all of the dimensions mentioned above, the one which seems the most relevant to dissent toleration is Moos' "social organizational climate," essentially equivalent to Inkeles and Levinson's "social process characteristics." In Moos' (1973a, 1974) work with nine different types of organizations (including the school), he has identified three broad types of social climate dimensions: 1) Relationship dimensions; 2) Personal development or personal growth dimensions; and 3) System maintenance and system change dimensions.

Briefly described, the relationship dimensions assess the "nature and intensity of personal relationships within the environment" (p. 11). The personal development dimensions concern the "basic directions along which personal growth and self-enhancement tend to occur in the particular environment" (p. 13). System maintenance and system change are dimensions which assess the "extent to which the environment is orderly, clear in its expectations, maintains control and is responsive to change" (pp. 13–14).

The best method for measuring such dimensions is a matter of some controversy. Some researchers (Withall, 1949; Medley and Mitzel, 1958; Flanders, 1970) emphasize the importance of observation techniques, maintaining that "low-inference" methods (i.e., counting discrete behaviors) are more objective and less subject to observation error. Others (Moos, 1973b; Walberg, 1974) have pointed out the advantage of using self-report questionnaires (i.e., student perceptions). Although such measures are less objective (i.e., they are "high inference" measures), they are judged to be better predictors of attitudinal outcomes. Moos (1973b) conjectures that this may be true, "since it is the global impressions which individuals remember and take into account in making major decisions about their lives" (p. 29). In comparing observation techniques with student self-reports, Anderson and Walberg (1974) maintain this about the student respondent:

Compared with a short-term observer, he weights in his judgment not only the class as it presently is but how it has been since the beginning of the year. He is able to compare from the child-client point of view his class with those in past grades or perhaps with others he is presently taking or even of other small groups of which he is a member. He and his classmates form a group of 20 to 30 sensitive, well-informed judges of the class; an outside observer is a single judge who has far less data and, though highly trained and systematic, may be insensitive to what is important in a particular class. (p. 86)

In constructing the measures for social climate, student perceptions from the IEA questionnaire were used. In addition, the following procedures, suggested by Wolf (1974) and paraphrased by McDill and Rigsby (1973) were adopted:

1. Select attributes of the (school) environment which earlier research and theory suggest have direct effects on the development of specific characteristics (achievement and aspirations) of members.

2. Summarize and treat the environmental data through the use of psychometric procedures. It is important to obtain information on several different conditions of

the environment and then to combine them in a systematic manner. As Wolf puts it, "A summarization of a number of variables is as important in describing an environment as a number of test items is in describing a student's competence in a subject."

3. Systematically relate the measures of environment to measures of individuals, as this provides one test of the validity of the measures of environment. (This guideline involves what we refer to as contextual analysis.) (McDill and Rigsby, p. 36—37)

The theoretical framework adopted for use in this study is that developed by Moos (1974). From the student questionnaires, it was possible to identify the following dimensions within Moos' three broad categories:

Relationship Dimensions
1. Classroom Equality
2. Peer Group Interaction

Personal Development Dimensions
3. Independence of Thought
4. Academic Climate
5. Political Environment
6. Ritual Climate

System Maintenance and System Change
7. Teacher Control
8. Student Power

Brief descriptions of each of these dimensions follow.

Classroom Equality
One of the most popular concepts in classroom climate research has been the notion of "openness." Weiler and Grossman (1973) hypothesize that classroom openness is related to dissent toleration. To them, an open educational climate is one that maximizes diversity, equality and tentativeness. Within the IEA data set are several measures of classroom equality which were appropriate for testing this aspect of classroom openness. These items were taken from Walberg and Anderson's (1968) Learning Environment Inventory (LEI), which has been widely used as the predictor of learning outcomes. Walberg and Anderson (1968) have shown that among other things, this dimension of climate is related to interest in science. It is thus included as one dimension of the school social climate in this study.

Peer Group Interaction
Drawing from the work of Merton and Kitt (1950) on "reference groups" and Coleman (1961) on the "adolescent society," McDill and Rigsby (1973) set out to show how certain aspects of peer group interactions have

an impact on student learning and attitudes. They consider peer group norms and pressures to be a central aspect of the school climate. Their study among some 18,000 high school students in the United States revealed the importance of peer group influences in determining a student's aspirations for higher education. In the present study, the number of peer group measures used was limited by the data set. The only peer group measures available were questions relating to the ways in which a student's group made decisions in specific situations, i.e., by voting or by some other method. In the early stages of this analysis, these items were used as conditioning variables. In later stages, they were incorporated into the school climate scale.

Independence of Thought

This could also be considered an aspect of classroom openness. The items entering this dimension are also taken from Walberg and Anderson's (1968) Learning Environment Inventory (LEI). The LEI subscale from which they come is called "diversity," which is another element of Weiler and Grossman's (1973) conceptualization of openness. In Torney, Oppenheim and Farnen (1975), this set of items is combined into a scale which they call "Encouragement of student independence in classroom." This variable was found to be significantly related to a low score on their measure of authoritarianism. Since the items all have to do with student thought and opinions, the dimension is referred to in this study as "Independence of Thought," and is considered to be an aspect of personal development.

Academic Climate

In Inkeles and Levinson's (1963) analytical framework, "qualities of mind" was cited as an important social process characteristic of an organization with a potential for influencing role performance. This aspect of the environment has been investigated by many researchers under the heading "cognitive climate" (Guilford, 1956; Gallagher, 1970; Steele, House and Kerins, 1971; Siegel and Siegel, 1967). Many of such studies draw upon Guilford's (1956) concept of five cognitive processes: memory, cognition, convergent and divergent production and evaluation. Others are based on a similar taxonomy by Bloom (1956). Of particular interest to this study is Steele, House and Kerin's study (1971), which measures the effects of "higher" vs. "lower" thought processes. Also relevant is the study by Zellman and Sears (1971) which related dissent toleration to "divergent thinking self-esteem." The IEA data set contains several measures of the student's perceptions of academic climate of their classes. These items are mainly concerned with the extent to which rote learning, as opposed to concept learning, is stressed in the classroom.

Political Environment

Gillespie and Ehman (1974) stress the importance of focusing on the systematic aspects of school political life. Ehman's 1969 study used a classroom climate measure composed of five politically relevant aspects: 1) teacher treatment of controversial issues; 2) teacher objectivity; 3) teacher neutrality; 4) discussion climate; and 5) teacher discussion of racial problems. Those classrooms in which the free and open discussion of controversial issues was common were considered "open;" those where there was little issue discussion were considered "closed." This measure of political climate was found to be significantly correlated with individual political orientations such as political efficacy. The IEA data set contains several measures of this nature. Some of these measures are teacher reports on the appropriateness of their arguing for certain controversial points of view. Another item, from the student's frame of reference, indicates how frequently students bring up current events. These items are considered to contribute to student development and are thus included in this domain of social climate.

Ritual Climate

Closely related to the preceding dimension is the ritual climate of a classroom. In fact, this dimension could be considered another facet of the political environment. Rituals such as the flag salute or singing nationalistic songs are not so much related to political cognitions and principles as they are to emotions and symbols. As such, they could be highly relevant to the domain of tolerance and nonconformity. Political symbols have always been endowed with a semi-sacred aura. Groups which place a high value on symbols and rituals are likely to react with a certain degree of irrationality towards cases of disrespect or disloyalty (e.g., flag burning in the United States).

A set of items asking about patriotic rituals were included in the IEA survey. These have been analyzed already in connection with authoritarian attitudes. Torney, Oppenheim and Farnen (1975) found that the practice of patriotic rituals was positively correlated with authoritarian attitudes at the Population II level in all eight countries. This same set of items is included as part of the social climate domain in an attempt to predict differences in dissent toleration.

Teacher Control

This dimension is designed to assess the extent to which the teachers exercise control over the thought and movement of the students. This dimension is perhaps the oldest and most examined area in school climate research. In the early years of school climate research, it appeared to be the only dimension of interest. Wrightstone (1934) developed a research instrument which categorized teacher behavior as either "integrative" or "dominative." This concept was further refined by Withall (1949), whose work led hundreds of researchers to categorize teachers' verbal behavior as either "teacher-centered" or "learner-centered." In recent years, this dimension has been perceived as only one aspect of the social climate of schooling. For example, Trickett and Moos (1973) developed an instrument called the Classroom Environment Scale (CES) in which Teacher Control is placed as one of nine different dimensions.

In the present study, this dimension is included as part of social climate, but as above, is only one of many (8) dimensions. The IEA data set contains several interesting items for assessing this dimension.

Student Power

This dimension is part of what other researchers have called organizational climate. It assesses the degree to which students are involved in decision making in the school. Organization Climate has been studied by many researchers (Andrews, 1965; Gentry and Kenney, 1965) using the Halpin and Croft (1963) Organizational Climate Description Questionnaire (OCDQ). Indicative of the times is the fact that this questionnaire contained no reference whatsoever to student participation in the organizational structure. It was the work of Bachman and his associates (1967) which focused attention on student (as well as faculty, administration and community) influence in school decision making. Wittes (1972) applied Bachman's ideas in developing an instrument to measure the power structure of the school. His research indicates that in schools where students are involved in decision making, they develop a greater sense of "internal control" and consequently exhibit higher levels of political efficacy.

Since student power was also considered to be relevant to the development of conflict norms, the IEA data set was searched for appropriate items. No appropriate student response items were found. However, a few relevant items were found in the school questionnaire, so this dimension was also included as part of school social climate.

Other Dimensions

Many other dimensions were considered during the early phases of mapping out the conceptual space of school social climate. Some aspects of student-student interactions were eliminated from consideration for the simple reason that the appropriate information had not been collected by IEA. Another dimension, referred to as socioeconomic context, was eliminated

55

on theoretical grounds. McDill and Rigsby (1973) had worked with this variable, using the average SES of the respondents in a school as the contextual variable. They found that this variable did not discriminate well between schools in math achievement and college aspirations. They concluded that SES context was not a very rigorous indicator of shared expectations and incentives among students, and suggested that "direct measures of organizational climate should be utilized in contextual analysis whenever possible" (p. 70). Since there were direct measures available in the data set, SES context was considered to be superfluous.

Constructing Subscales

After the dimensions of social climate were chosen and defined and appropriate indicators of the dimensions were located in the data set, the next step was to summarize and treat the environmental data through the use of psychometric procedures. In the case of the individual dimensions, this meant trying to build subscales using the available items.

Some work in this area had already been done by Torney, Oppenheim and Farnen (1975). Three dimensions, Classroom Equality, Independence of Thought, and Ritual Climate, had already been scaled and reliability coefficients of respectable strengths had been found.[1] The median alpha reliabilities for each of the scales over nine IEA countries were, respectively, .581, .650, and .533. Another dimension, Peer Group Interaction, was constructed such that four items, each of them situations where voting might be called for, were combined into one composite variable. Item analysis shows this variable to be well distributed in both countries of interest, the mean scores on a 5 point scale being 2.93 in the USA; 3.19 in the FRG.

The other independent variable dimension presented problems in scaling. The general pattern was that of very low or negative intercorrelations of the items. For example, there were six items chosen to represent Academic Climate. One half of these items were student perceptions of the cognitive level of the instruction. The other half were teacher reports on teaching behaviors (i.e., methods of evaluation). In the USA, only two variables were intercorrelated with a coefficient greater than .10. The item "Great stress on facts in civics class" had a correlation of .20 with "Must learn dates, etc. by heart." "Use of printed drill" was negatively correlated ($-.14$) with "Student assessment: projects and papers." In the FRG, only one correlation was greater than .10, the one between "Student assessment: projects and papers" and "Student assessment: essay tests" ($r=.21$). Faced with such weak correlations, further attempts to scale the items were abandoned. Instead, a decision was made to include the strongest item from this item

---

[1] The items included in these subscales are listed in the Appendix, part D.

pool to represent the dimension. The procedures for doing this are discussed in the next section.

Similar problems were encountered in trying to scale the Political Environment items. An examination of the matrix of intercorrelations revealed the same pattern of low or negative correlations. In addition, another problem was observed. There was almost no correlation between the student perception variables and the teacher variables. This phenomenon was observed every time teacher variables were combined with student level variables. The most reasonable explanation for this phenomenon is the fact that the teachers sampled were not necessarily the teachers of the students sampled from a school. In addition, the data reveals that in the United States over half of the schools sampled only one teacher. On the basis of these observations (plus later results from a factor analysis), teacher variables were eliminated from the school climates variable pool. With respect to the Political Environment measure, this left only one item, the item "Students bring up current events."

With respect to the Teacher Control variable, the same pattern emerged once again. None of the intercorrelations were greater than .13 in either country. However, since in the United States all but one of the correlations were positive, reliability coefficients were computed. The KR-20 reliability coefficients for the subscale in the United States and the Federal Republic were .237 and .094 respectively, hardly high enough to warrant using the items together as a subscale.

Finally, similar results were obtained when attempts were made to scale the Student Power items. Unfortunately, the items were indirect ones to begin with, that is, taken from the teacher or the school questionnaires. The patterns of intercorrelations between the items were similar to previous patterns: low correlations with mixed signs. Once again, the decision was made to represent this dimension with a single best item.

Choosing Items

Since for four of the eight dimensions, subscales could not be formed, the best items had to be chosen in some way to represent these climate dimensions. Two different approaches were taken. The first could be referred to as "hand-picking." This approach considered the content of the item (i.e., whether it represented the concept well) and the item's correlation with the criterion, Dissent Toleration. Under this approach, care was taken to choose items which were relatively strong in both countries. Since a quasi-criterion scaling method was being employed here, one of the subscales was reexamined. The Classroom Equality Scale was not significantly correlated with DISTOL 4D. However, one item in the dimension pool was. This item was thus "hand-picked" to represent the dimension in this phase of scale construction. The following items were hand-picked to represent the five climate dimensions which were not represented by subscales. Table 4.2 gives the items and their correlations with the scale DISTOL 4D.

Table 4.2 Hand-Picked Items and Their Correlations with DISTOL 4D

Dimension	Item	Correlation with DISTOL 4D USA	FRG
Academic Climate	Causes and explanations are stressed before names and dates	.23	.31
Political Environment	Students bring up current events	.12	.04
Teacher Control	Students agree with teacher	.13	.18
Student Power	Students make school policies	.08	.11
Classroom Equality	Every class member has same privileges	.08	.08

The other procedure employed in choosing items was factor analysis. The hand-picking procedure could be seen as giving unfair advantage to the climate items relative to other variables in the model which were not chosen on the basis of their correlations with the criterion. To avoid charges of contamination, the climate items were factor analyzed in order to maximize their internal coherence and not their correlation with Dissent Toleration. The principal component solution was utilized. All of the relevant items, including the teacher items, were entered. Several selection standards were considered. Finally, the decision was made to select one item (or item group) with the highest factor loading within each dimension.[2] This meant that the items would not necessarily be the same in both countries. The items selected according to this criterion (plus the scales already selected) and their factor loadings are presented in Table 4.3.

Constructing the School Social Climate Scales

Three different climate scales (CLIME 1, CLIME 2, CLIME 3) were created, each drawing upon a different set of items. In all cases, the item or scale representing a dimension was standardized (z-scored) before being combined with the other items or scales. The first version of the scale

---

[2] This decision meant that some of the items had very low loadings. However, the theoretical justification for including at least one item from each dimension was strong enough that this weakness was tolerated. See also the discussion on heterogeneous scales on p. 60.

Table 4.3   Factor Analyzed Social Climate Items

	USA		FRG	
Dimension	Item	Factor Loading	Item	Factor Loading
Academic Climate	Causes and explanations before names, dates	.29	Must learn dates, etc. by heart	.33
Political Environment	Students bring up current events	.33	Students bring up current events	.27
Teacher Control	Teachers make you feel small[r]	.49	Teachers make you feel small[r]	.52
Student Power	Student participation in discipline	.05	Students make school policies	.02
Classroom Equality	Scale composition: 1. Every class member has some privileges 2. Better students get special favors[r] 3. Certain students are more favored than rest[r]	.60	Scale composition: 1. Every class member has same privileges 2. Better students get special favors[r] 3. Certain students are more favored than rest[r]	.65
Independence of Thought	Subscale[a]	.65	Subscale[a]	.59
Ritual Climate	Subscale[r,a]	−.21	Subscale[r,a]	.18
Peer Group Interaction	Subscale[a]	.17	Subscale[a]	.08

[r] Indicates reverse coding.
[a] Subscale items are listed in the Appendix, part D.

(CLIME 1) used the hand-picked items from among the eight climate dimensions. This scale was used in many of the early analyses. The second version of the scale (CLIME 2) used the hand-picked items again, but only included seven climate dimensions. The dimension covering Peer Group Interaction (PGI) was excluded in this version, under the assumption that PGI might tap a social environment somewhat removed from that of the school. In this case, PGI was used as a conditioning variable. In later stages of the analysis, it was decided that cases where members of a student's peer group were different than his school mates would be very rare at age 14; consequently, the version CLIME 2 was not used further.

Finally, CLIME 3 was constructed using the factor analyzed items for each country. This version was considered to be the "cleanest" form of the scale, since no reference to the criterion was made until after the scale was constructed.

It should be noted that in the case of the United States, the two versions of the scale most utilized, CLIME 1 and CLIME 3, were essentially equivalent. That is, the hand-picked scale was essentially the same as the factor analyzed scale. There were only two items (and parts of a third) which differed between the two versions of the scale. The correlation between CLIME 1 and CLIME 3 was .94.

In the case of the Federal Republic, the picture is quite different. Although the two versions of the scale differ on the same number of items as in the United States, the distance between the differing items was substantial. Thus, the correlation between CLIME 1 and CLIME 3 was only .72. Clearly, these are not equivalent scales. This means, among other things, that the analyses using CLIME 1 for the Federal Republic have to be interpreted with some caution.[3]

Generally when describing a scale one would report on its internal consistency and on its test-retest reliability. The social climate scales constructed for this study are heterogeneous scales, in which different parts measure different "traits" of the environment. As such, according to Guilford and Fruchter (1973, p. 407), the items cannot be expected to be very highly inter-correlated and hence internal consistency is not a very meaningful concept. In fact, the items of the social climate scales are generally either weakly- or uncorrelated with each other. Thus internal consistency coefficients were not even computed for these scales. Furthermore, since data were collected only on one occasion, it was not possible to compute a test-retest reliability coefficient.

Thus the usefulness of the scale was determined primarily on the basis of its validity. The fact that the scales themselves were generally more highly correlated with dissent toleration than any of their constituent items were,

---

[3] Actually, caution is required only when using CLIME 1 in competition with other variables as a predictor, since in the construction of the other variables their correlations with Dissent Toleration were not taken into consideration. This would tend to give CLIME 1 an advantage from the beginning. Used by itself, however, there is no reason why CLIME 1 should be any less valid than CLIME 3. The advantage of the latter over the former is that it better meets standards of "internal consistency." However, in the paragraphs which follow, I will show that internal consistency is a relatively meaningless concept for heterogeneous scales, which is what this scale is. The advantage of CLIME 1 on the other hand is that it contains some items from the pool which, though not as consistent with the scale as others, are nevertheless conceptually more relevant to Dissent Toleration. (For example: "Students agree with the teacher" (CLIME 1) as opposed to "Teachers make you feel small" (CLIME 3).) Thus, while CLIME 3 is cleaner empirically, CLIME 1 is a conceptually more powerful scale. Since both empirical and conceptual standards are important, I have chosen to present the results using both versions of the scale.

argues for their relatively strong predictive validity and their usefulness as predictors. (See Table 5.3)

The above work completes the second procedure of the three suggested by Wolf. The third, relating environment measures to individual measures will be the main concern of Chapter 5.

Operationalizing the Conditioning Variables

Antecedent Conditions

The first of the antecedent variables, student sex, was determined from the student's response to a questionnaire item. Ethnicity, a variable of theoretical interest, was not operationalizable, since IEA did not ask individuals to state their ethnic identity.

Cognitive ability was measured through the use of a verbal aptitude test constructed by IEA especially for its cross-national surveys. The Word Knowledge Test consisted of 40 pairs of words which were either alike or nearly opposite in meaning. The student was to indicate whether the pair was one or the other. His or her responses were corrected for guessing (see Choppin, 1974). The test was developed first in English and then translated into the other languages. Pretests were conducted in order to verify the quality of the translations. The development and use of the corrected Word Knowledge Test is further discussed in Thorndike (1973).

The conditioning variable "type of program" was operationalized by using the information from a single questionnaire item which asked students to indicate the type of academic course they were following. The responses were precoded according to the unique properties of the respective national education systems. In the United States, the alternatives were: 1) General education, 2) Vocational/commercial education, or 3) Academic education. In the Federal Republic, the alternatives were: 1) *Hauptschule* (a terminal extension of primary school), 2) *Realschule* (an intermediate, vocationally oriented school), and 3) the *Gymnasium* (the academic, university preparatory school).

The last antecedent conditioning variable is social class background. This was operationalized along rather conventional lines using father's education (in years), mother's education (in years) and father's occupation (grouped by the categories unskilled and semi-skilled; skilled and clerical; professional and managerial) in an index. In order not to overrepresent education in the index, father's occupation was given a weight of 2; the education variables were weighted one each.

Concurrent Conditions

The two concurrent conditions thought to be relevant to the model were religious activity and conflict with the family. The first was taken from a single item on the questionnaire. The youth were asked to indicate if they had joined in church activities. They could answer "Never thought of it," "Thought about it, but haven't done it," or "Have done it." The responses were dichotomized so that "have done it" was given the value of 1; the other two responses, zero.

Conflict with the family was measured using several items from the student questionnaire. The index measures the extent to which youth consider themselves independent of or in conflict with their parents or elders. The index consists of two items which measure political disagreement with parents and three others which assess the extent to which the student does things that "older people don't approve of." A test of scalability shows this "scale" to have alpha reliabilities of .34 in the USA and .59 in the FRG.

Anticipatory Conditions

Educational aspirations was the single anticipatory conditions variable in this study. Two items were available in the IEA survey which related to this dimension. First was an agree/disagree question, "I hope to study at a university." The second asked for student educational *expectations* in years. The two items were by no means identical. Their zero-order correlation in the USA was .45; in the FRG .50. Although the former item was more directly related to the theoretical literature on university aspirations, the latter item showed higher levels of association with other variables in the study, such as Civics Achievement and Word Knowledge. This is perhaps partly due to the fact that the university aspirations item is phrased in a rather imprecise manner. "Hope to study at the university" may tap unrealistic fantasies as well as concrete plans. On the basis of these considerations, the educational expectations item (years) was chosen for use in the present study.

Measuring Civics Knowledge

The model elaborated in Chapter 2 showed how dissent toleration was expected to be related to knowledge of democratic principles. In turn, it showed an expectation that such knowledge would be influenced by the social climate of schooling. Thus, Civics Knowledge was placed in the model as an intervening variable between School Social Climate and Dissent Toleration. Chapter 3 has gone into some detail to describe how the Civics Cognitive Test was constructed. This test was used here without modification (except for the correction for guessing—see Choppin, 1974). The 47 item test was found to be highly reliable in both the United States and the Federal Republic, the KR-20 reliability coefficients being .877 and .861, respectively.

Summary

This chapter has outlined in some detail how each of the variables in the research model was operationalized using IEA data. In most cases, certain compromises had to be made between what would have been the ideal operationalization of a concept and what the data set would allow. The main dependent variable, Dissent Toleration, was represented by the scale DISTOL 4D, which consisted of 11 items drawn from the IEA factors Tolerance and Support for Civil Liberties, Belief in the Value of Criticism of Government, and Active Perception of Citizenship.

The main independent variable, School Social Climate, was operationalized according to the conceptual scheme of Moos (1974). Dimensions were found in the IEA data which fit into Moos' three dimension types: Relationship Dimensions, Personal Development Dimensions, and System Maintenance and Change Dimensions. Measures were chosen from a pool of items for each dimension according to two methods, "handpicking" and factor analysis. Scales (CLIME 1 and CLIME 3) were constructed using the items and subscales selected. The two versions of the scale for the United States were essentially equivalent. The two versions for the Federal Republic were rather different and the effects of this on the analysis will be noted.

The conditioning variables in the model were of three types: antecedent, concurrent and anticipatory. All but one variable, ethnicity, could be adequately operationalized using IEA data. The intervening variable, Civics Knowledge, was measured using the Cognitive Civics Test, which was a highly reliable instrument designed especially for IEA research.

Chapter 5

The Analyses

Preliminary Considerations

The main argument of this thesis is that the social climate of schooling is related to the development of dissent toleration in youth. Two different kinds of processes are thought to be operating. First, there are organizational effects on the student's "personality structure." Such effects occur as the result of indirect political socialization processes, particularly "interpersonal transference." In this process, the patterning of activities and tasks in an organization (e.g., whether they are rigid or flexible) can have an influence on the patterning of individual thinking and behavior (e.g., rigid or flexible). Thus, the social climate of schooling is thought to have a direct impact on the part of dissent toleration which is related to "personality structure." The other process involves the "idea system" of the student. The assumption is that students who know more about the principles of democracy (the "democratic creed") will accept and practice the essential democratic ideal of tolerance. In addition, those who have gained some familiarity with minority groups' problems and aims should be more disposed to tolerate their challenges to the system. To the extent that the social climate of schooling enhances learning in these areas, it has an indirect effect on dissent toleration as well as a direct effect.

Simple correlational analysis would give some indication as to whether or not the hypothesized relationships were present in the empirical world. Yet, with so many other spheres of influence acting at the same time, without some kind of statistical controls it would not be possible to affirm that the main variables were *independently* related. In other words, certain personal attributes such as cognitive ability, aspirations, or family background could be more important in explaining dissent toleration than school climate. They could also be related to the kind of social climate the student was exposed to. To the extent that they are related both to the criterion and to the main independent variable, they could attenuate what was seen on the basis of simple correlations to be a substantial relationship between the two.

There are several ways to statistically control the impact of conditioning variables. Besides the relatively simple procedures of cross-tabulation and partial correlation, the more powerful tool of multiple regression is often used. In the analyses which follow, simple correlation and multiple regression techniques will be employed, with emphasis given to the regression analysis. At the end, some exercises in path modelling will be presented, in order to suggest ways in which the variables are causally related.

Before getting into the bivariate and multivariate analyses, some preliminary issues will be taken up for purposes of clarification and description. In the area of clarification, two issues, the unit of analysis and methods of between-country comparisons, will be raised. By way of description, a brief section outlining the central tendency of the important variables will be presented.

Unit of Analysis

There has been considerable controversy over which unit of analysis, the individual or the group, is most appropriate for social climate research. Some researchers (Pace and Stern, 1958), conceiving social climate to be basically the attribute of an organization, prefer to work with group data. Others (Pervin, 1968), more concerned with individuals and their perceived environments, have relied more heavily on individual perceptions. Still others (Anderson and Walberg, 1974) have used both individual and group data in demonstrating environmental impacts.

One advantage of group data is that it presents a *consensus* of environment perception which approaches the degree of objectivity which outside observers might attain. Aggregated perceptions can then be used as predictors of group outcomes. Yet what if the interest is in the attitudes, values or behaviors of individuals? Robinson (1950) has pursuasively argued that group level findings cannot be generalized to individuals.

This study is concerned with individual level outcomes, for it is more meaningful to talk about a tolerant individual than a tolerant classroom. Clearly, then, individual data is called for in the case of the dependent variable, But what can be said about the social climate measure?

If it could be demonstrated that individual perceptions of environments are relatively consistent or stable across individuals, then there would be little danger in using individual data. Some critics, however, have maintained that environment perceptions may be more strongly related to personal characteristics than to external conditions. Thus, correlations between an individual environment measure and an outcome measure might reflect the existence of an underlying personal tendency to respond in basically the same ways to both stimuli. For example, a person may have a positive perception of a social climate because he is basically an optimistic person, a fact which also causes him to respond in a positive way to a set of statements about political tolerance. In this situation, more is said about a "perceptual tendency" than the *influence* of social climate on tolerance.

In recent years researchers have begun to address this issue. Stern

(1964), Walberg and Anderson (1968), Moos and Bromet (1976) have presented evidence that individual perceptions of environments are not related in any consistent way to personal characteristics. Some of these same researchers have suggested ways in which safeguards against the perceptual tendency problem can be built into the analytical design. Anderson (1970) demonstrated that an integrated analysis could be conducted, using both individual and group data. In this design, the outcome measure remained at the individual level, but the social environment was treated as an aggregate measure, each member of the group (classroom) being assigned the mean perception score for his group. Mean perceptions were then correlated with individual outcomes.

Another approach suggested by Moos[1] would be to divide the sample in half, correlating the environment perception measures of one half of the group with the outcome measures of the other half.

In this study I will use primarily individual level data. However, in order to guard against possible contamination because of perceptual tendency I will conduct one phase of the analysis using aggregated perception scores, in much the same way that Anderson (1970) did. This integrated analysis I will refer to as a "contextual analysis."

Between Country Comparisons

Of particular interest in this study are the *processes* by which schools influence political thinking in American and West German youth. Of less interest, in fact hardly commented upon, are the absolute differences between the two countries on the various scales. In other words, the attempt here is to determine how and to what extent school climates influence dissent toleration and to see if these influences can be generalized to more than one industrialized country. The study is not interested in showing why one country appears to make a better showing on a particular test than another. Between country differences in scores will only be mentioned in passing.

Since this study calls for cross-national comparisons it is important to consider the trade-offs between using *identical* and *equivalent* measures.[2] The Dissent Toleration scale constructed for this research uses identical measures in the two countries. This is justified by the fact that the questions deal with hypothetical situations thought by the IEA committee to be salient in all participating countries. The school climate measures were con-

---

[1] Personal Communication, October, 1975.

[2] Identical measures are exactly the same across countries to the extent that different languages allow. Equivalent measures have a core of identical items but allow for local variations. For a thorough description of the differences between them see Przeworski and Teune (1970).

structed in two different ways: first with identical measures and then with equivalent measures. The previous chapter showed in some detail why and how the two versions of the scale were constructed. This chapter reports on the analyses using both versions. The relative merits of the two approaches will be discussed later in the chapter.

Descriptive Statistics

Table 5.1 lists the mean scores of the dependent variable items and scale for the United States and the Federal Republic. Mean scores are higher on all

Table 5.1 Mean Values for Dissent Toleration -- USA and FRG

Item		Mean Score* USA	Mean Score* FRG	Standard Dev USA	Standard Dev FRG
1.	Newspapers should be allowed to print anything	.547	.740	.498	.439
2.	People should be allowed to come together whenever they like	.777	.812	.416	.391
3.	Citizens must always be free to criticize the government	.743	.873	.437	.333
4.	People who disagree with gov't allowed to meet and protest	.509	.614	.500	.487
5.	When something wrong, better to complain than to keep quiet	.789	.850	.408	.358
6.	It is good for the government to be frequently criticized	.580	.641	.494	.480
7.	The people in power know best[r]	.661	.721	.473	.449
8.	It is wrong to criticize our government[r]	.694	.673	.461	.469
9.	People should not criticize the gov't, it only interrupts work[r]	.722	.758	.448	.428
10.	Rights of people with anti-national views	.628	.771	.483	.420
11.	A good citizen tries to change things in government	.745	.569	.436	.495
	OVERALL SCALE (DISTOL 4D)	.671	.730	.046	.037
	Number of Students USA: 3111 FRG: 1275				

* All items are dichotomous, such that the scores fall between 0 and 1.

[r] Indicates reverse coding.

items in the Federal Republic except in two cases. The fact that the West German students score lower on the item "A good citizen tries to change things in government" probably indicates more about West Germans' attitudes towards active political participation than about their attitudes towards dissent.

The overall scale scores are more interesting when put in a broader context. The score for the Federal Republic was the highest of all the scores for the eight IEA countries. The score for the United States ranked fourth behind those for the Federal Republic of Germany, Ireland and New Zealand. Although this finding for the United States challenges the notion common among Americans that they live in the freest, most open society in the world, it also gives some encouragement to those who pessimistically reported a decline in support for civil liberties during the 1950's.[3] With respect to West Germany, these scores suggest that the decade of the Sixties went a long way towards correcting in youth what Dahrendorf (1967) termed "a fallacious attitude toward conflict in politics" (p. 140).

Table 5.2 gives the mean scores for the independent and conditioning variables. Since the main objective of this research is not to compare raw scores, only a few highlights from the table will be commented upon here. An overview of the social climate variables reveals that in six of eight climate dimensions, West German students report more positive (according to the scoring scheme of this study) conditions. West German students report very low levels of patriotic ritual in their classes and very high levels of classroom equality. American students report higher levels of student initiative in bringing up current events and a generally higher propensity to disagree with teachers. With respect to the conditioning and intervening variables, a few interesting differences emerge. American 14-year-olds appear to be, on the average, both more involved in religious activities and more in conflict with their parents than West German students. The status variables are hard to compare. Generally speaking, education levels are higher for students from the United States, both in terms of their parents' achieved education and their own education expectations. But these variables cannot be directly compared since the education profiles in the two countries are so different. On the intervening variable, Civics Knowledge, West German youth achieve somewhat better scores than the American youth.

---

[3] See Remmers (1963), p. 62. One question included in the IEA survey is identical to one used by Remmers et al. in their 1951 and 1960 surveys, namely: "Newspapers and magazines should be allowed to print anything they want except military secrets." The percentages agreeing with this statement for the three years (including 1971, the year of the IEA Survey) are as follows: 1951, 45%; 1960, 29%; 1971, 55% (IEA).

Table 5.2 Mean Scores for Independent and Conditioning Variables—USA and FRG

School Social Climate Variables	USA	FRG	Possible Range
Causes and explanations before names, dates	3.62	3.66	1 – 5
Must learn dates, etc. by heart[a]	----	3.36	1 – 5
Students bring up current events	3.39	2.74	1 – 5
Students agree with teacher (reverse coding)	0.78	0.66	0 – 1
Teachers make you feel small (reverse coding)	0.53	0.54	0 – 1
Students make school policies	0.97	1.16	1 – 3
Student participation in discipline[b]	0.66	----	0 – 1
Every class member has same privileges	3.56	4.18	1 – 5
Classroom Equality Scale	2.89	3.58	1 – 5
Independence of Thought Scale	3.76	3.99	1 – 5
Ritual Climate Scale (reverse coding)	2.28	1.58	1 – 5
Peer Group Interaction Scale	2.93	3.19	1 – 5
Conditioning Variables			
Student Sex	1.48	1.48	1 – 2
Word Knowledge[c]	16.30	14.31	1 – 40
Type of Program	1.96	1.54	1 – 3
Father's Education[d]	3.88	3.16	1 – 5
Mother's Education[d]	3.82	3.04	1 – 5
Father's Occupation	2.55	2.01	1 – 3
Religious Activity	2.19	1.46	1 – 3
Conflict with the Family	1.90	1.62	.6 – 3
Educational Expectations[e]	3.79	2.43	1 – 5
Intervening Variable			
Civics Knowledge	24.68	26.01	−11.8 to 47

[a] Used in the FRG only.

[b] Used in the USA only.

[c] Since the Word Knowledge test was not identical in the two countries, these results should not be compared.

[d] Categories as follows: 1 = 0 years; 2 = greater than 0, less than or equal to 5 years; 3 = greater than 5, less than or equal to 10 years; 4 = greater than 10, less than or equal to 15 years; 5 = greater than 15 years.

[e] Categories as follows: 1 = 0 additional years; 2 = greater than 0, less than or equal to 2 years; 3 = greater than 2, less than or equal to 5 years; 4 = greater than 5, less than or equal to 8; 5 = greater than 8 additional years.

Zero-Order Correlations with Dissent Toleration

The Pearson product-moment correlation formula was used to determine "zero-order" relationships between the variables. The term zero-order is

Table 5.3 Zero-order Correlations between School Social Climate Variables and Dissent Toleration -- USA and FRG

Social Climate Dimension	Item	Correlation[c] USA	FRG
Classroom Equality	a) Every class member has same privileges	.082*	.083*
	b) Classroom Equality Scale	.028	−.040
Peer Group Interaction	c) Peer Group Interaction Scale	.128*	.193*
Independence of Thought	d) Independence of Thought Scale	.086*	.201*
Academic Climate	e) Causes and explanations before names and dates	.233*	.306*
	f) Must learn dates, etc. by heart[a]	----	.013
Political Environment	g) Students bring up current events	.121*	.040
Ritual Climate	h) Ritual Climate Scale	−.102*	−.201*
Teacher Control	i) Students agree with teacher	.134*	.184*
	j) Teachers make you feel small	.037	.036
Student Power	k) Students make school policies	.085*	.110*
	l) Student participation in discipline[b]	−.001	----
CLIME 1	(a, c, d, e, g, h, i, k)	.271*	.392*
CLIME 3	USA (b, c, d, e, g, h, j, l)	.212*	
	FRG (b, c, d, f, g, h, j, k)		.171*

[a] Used in FRG only.
[b] Used in USA only.
[c] Correlations designated "*" are significant at the .001 level.

used because the correlation is a simple bivariate relationship, with no controls added. Table 5.3 shows the zero-order correlations between the school climate variables and Dissent Toleration (DISTOL 4D).

The table reveals several interesting findings. First, taking just CLIME 1 items, the hand-picked ones, it appears that all of the climate items but one, "Students bring up current events," are more strongly correlated with Dissent Toleration in the Federal Republic than in the United States. The strongest correlate with Dissent Toleration in both countries is "Causes and explanations stressed before names and dates." Also strong in the FRG compared with the USA are "Independence of Thought" and "Ritual Climate." The zero-order correlations between CLIME 1 and DISTOL 4D

(.271 in USA; .392 in FRG) give the impression that social climate is more strongly related to dissent toleration in the Federal Republic than in the United States.

When CLIME 3, the factor analyzed scale, is used, a different pattern appears. First of all, in each case and in both countries where the factor analysis called for substitution of one of the hand-picked items, the correlation of the new item with DISTOL was found to be statistically non-significant. In two cases in the FRG, a sign change occurred when items were substituted (from positive to negative). Consequently, the overall scale correlations, CLIME 3 with DISTOL 4D, were reduced. In the USA, the reduction in the correlation coefficient was relatively minor (.06); in the FRG the reduction was significant (.22). Although strictly speaking CLIME 3 is the cleaner version of the social climate scale, it presents a conservative estimate of the effects of social climate on dissent toleration, especially in the case of West Germany. On the other hand, the use of CLIME 1 would probably overestimate the impact of school social climate, especially in comparison with other variables, since they were not chosen by the criterion method. Disregarding magnitude of correlation for a moment, the problem could be seen in another way, that is, as a test of a hypothesis. The principal null hypothesis for this study would be: School climate does not influence the development of dissent toleration in 14-year-olds. If by using the most stringent tests (powerful control variables and the "cleanest" version of the school climate scale) the relationship between school social climate and dissent toleration does not disappear (become statistically non-significant), then the null hypothesis can be rejected and the alternative (that school social climate does influence the development of dissent toleration) can be affirmed.

This is one of the central aims of this study. The other is to show that school climates influence dissent toleration indirectly through their impacts on civics knowledge. Zero-order correlations with Civics Knowledge will be examined in the next section.

Zero-order Correlations with Civics Knowledge

The first zero-order relationships of interest here are those between Civics Knowledge and Dissent Toleration. They are as follows: for the USA, .470; for the FRG, .514. These are rather strong correlations and, of course, with such large N's are highly significant. One might argue that the two variables are measuring essentially the same thing. Yet the items for the two scales were developed by entirely different teams, starting from different frames of reference and with different goals in mind. Another interpretation could be that they both reflect the same capacity to take tests. However, the civics test was the only one on which the "right" answer was asked for. The Dissent Toleration scale was given as an attitude survey. A third interpretation could be that those who know more about democratic principles will recognize the part dissent toleration plays in a democracy and will incorporate it into their set of attitudes. This is the theoretical position which guided this research. Yet this agreement between preconceptions and empirical findings should not obscure the possibility of other causal orderings. It is feasible that persons who are more tolerant are able to score higher on civics achievement tests, possibly because their tolerance reflects greater interest in politics. There is, however, no compelling reason to accept this explanation above the previous. The matter of causal ordering will be further discussed in the path analysis section of this chapter and in Chapter 6.

The next link to consider with respect to the intervening variables is that between Civics Knowledge and the social climate variables. Table 5.4 shows the zero-order correlations between these variables. The most impressive correlations revealed by the table are those between the summary climate scale, CLIME 1 and Civics Knowledge. These correlations of .431 and .399 for the United States and the Federal Republic respectively are stronger than any of the climate correlations with Dissent Toleration. There is no danger of contamination in the use of the hand-picked scale in predicting Civics Knowledge since the scaling criterion was Dissent Toleration. CLIME 3 correlations with Civics Knowledge are given anyway, and, though somewhat reduced, they still are quite respectable. Overall, the relationship of School Social Climate to Civics Knowledge is stronger in the United States.

Looking at the climate items individually, some interesting patterns can be observed. As in the case when Dissent Toleration was the criterion, the Academic Climate item "Causes and explanations are stressed before names and dates" is the strongest correlate of Civics Knowledge. This is not surprising, since this test was composed to measure understanding of more abstract political ideas as opposed to historical facts. Other items which were relatively strong correlates of Civics Knowledge were Peer Group Interaction and "Students agree with teacher." These two items are not the kind of items one would expect to find *influencing* civics achievement. One way to account for their relatively strong correlation with Civics Knowledge is to think of them as characteristic of bright students, i.e., brighter students are more democratic in their peer group relationships and more prone to disagree with their teachers. In addition, bright students are those who are more likely to achieve high scores on the civics test. Controlling for scholastic aptitude, one could determine whether or not there was a relationship between these climate items and Civics Knowledge, independent of aptitude. Fortunately, such a measure, Word Knowledge, is

Table 5.4 Zero-order Correlations between School Social Climate Variables and Civics Knowledge -- USA and FRG

Social Climate Dimension	Item	Correlation[c] USA	FRG
Classroom Equality	a) Every class member has same privileges	.143*	.094*
	b) Classroom Equality Scale	−.046	−.016
Peer Group Interaction	c) Peer Group Interaction Scale	.204*	.296*
Independence of Thought	d) Independence of Thought Scale	.109*	.172*
Academic Climate	e) Causes and explanations before names and dates	.324*	.349*
	f) Must learn dates, etc. by heart[a]	----	.007
Political Environment	g) Students bring up current events	.154*	−.067*
Ritual Climate	h) Ritual Climate Scale	−.113*	−.245*
Teacher Control	i) Students agree with teacher	.260*	.236*
	j) Teachers make you feel small	.158*	.024
Student Power	k) Students make school policies	.169*	.084*
	l) Student participation in discipline[b]	−.027	----
CLIME 1	(a, c, d, e, g, h, i, k)	.431*	.399*
CLIME 3	USA (b,c, d, e, g, h, i, l)	.357*	
	FRG (b, c, d, f, g, h, j, k)		.216*

[a] Used in FRG only.
[b] Used in USA only.
[c] All correlations designated "*" are significant at the .001 level.

available as one of the conditioning variables. A report of the effects of operating such a control will appear later in the section entitled "Disaggregating the Effects of School Social Climate."

Figure 5.1 demonstrates that in both countries School Climate is both directly and indirectly (via Civics Knowledge) related to Dissent Toleration, at least in terms of simple correlations. The next step is to determine how well these relationships hold up when the conditioning variables are controlled. Before the results of this task are presented, some bivariate relationships involving the conditioning variables will be examined.

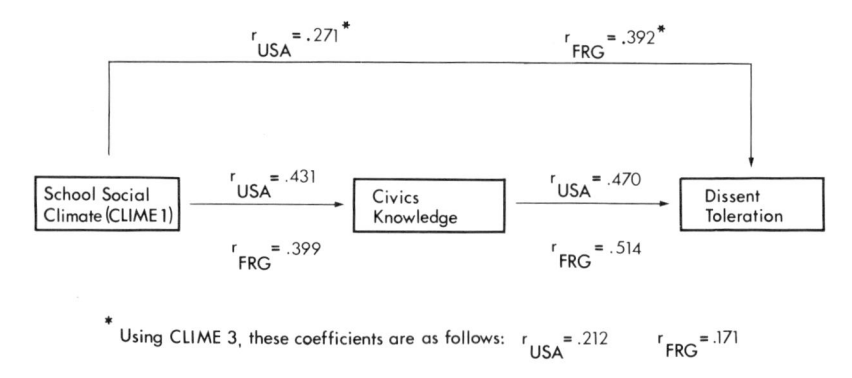

```
                r_USA = .271*                        r_FRG = .392*
     ┌──────────────────────────────────────────────────────────────┐
     │                                                              ▼
┌─────────────────┐   r_USA = .431   ┌───────────┐   r_USA = .470   ┌─────────────┐
│ School Social   │ ───────────────▶ │  Civics   │ ───────────────▶ │  Dissent    │
│ Climate (CLIME 1)│  r_FRG = .399   │ Knowledge │   r_FRG = .514   │ Toleration  │
└─────────────────┘                  └───────────┘                  └─────────────┘
```

* Using CLIME 3, these coefficients are as follows: $r_{USA} = .212$ $r_{FRG} = .171$

Figure 5.1. Zero-order Relationships between School Social Climate, Civics Knowledge and Dissent Toleration.

Zero-order Correlations with the Conditioning Variables

As indicated in Chapter 2, the conditioning variables chosen for use in this study were selected because they all were expected to be predictors of dissent toleration and thus to provide alternative explanations for the ways in which this orientation develops in adolescents. It is also expected that some of the conditioning variables will be related to the independent and intervening variables of the study, thus "conditioning" bivariate relationships between them and dissent toleration. Table 5.5 is a matrix which shows the zero-order correlations among the conditioning variables and between them and the other variables of this study. The table presents two asymmetrical matrices, that for the United States falling below the diagonal; that for the Federal Republic above it. The Parental SES variable is disaggregated here in order to provide more information.

One thing that becomes immediately apparent from the table is the fact that two conditioning variables, Student Sex and Religious Activities, are apparently uncorrelated with Dissent Toleration. The strongest correlation for each of these variables in both countries is that with the other. In other words, girls tend to be more involved in religious activities than boys in both countries. Student Sex tends to be related to Educational Expectations in both countries (boys having higher expectations in both) and Religious Activities appear to be slightly correlated with academic ability (the more able being somewhat more involved in religious activities). Apart from these interesting sidelights, the two conditioning variables in question appear to be basically unrelated to the variables in the model and will not be analyzed further.

The strongest correlations in the matrix are those between Word

Table 5.5 Correlation Matrix for Conditioning Variables, Social Climate (CLIME 1), Civics Knowledge and Dissent Toleration — USA and FRG

FRG

		C_1	C_{2a}	C_{2b}	C_{2c}	C_3	C_4	C_5	C_6	C_7	X_1	Z_1	Y_1
C_1	Student Sex		.03	.04	−.06	.06	−.02	.12[a]	−.00	−.09[a]	.09[b]	−.06	−.01
C_{2a}	Father's Education	−.03		.59[a]	.51[a]	.35[a]	.23[a]	.07[b]	.09[a]	.36[a]	.02	.19[a]	.15[a]
C_{2b}	Mother's Education	−.03	.60[a]		.21[a]	.31[a]	.20[a]	.11[a]	.08[b]	.20[a]	.00	.13[a]	.09[a]
C_{2c}	Father's Occupation	−.02	.39[a]	.27[a]		.29[a]	.18[a]	.02	.13[a]	.39[a]	.06	.27[a]	.16[a]
C_3	Word Knowledge	−.00	.25[a]	.15[a]	.30[a]		.59[a]	.04	.29[a]	.35[a]	.37[a]	.63[a]	.39[a]
C_4	Type of Program	.02	.36[a]	.22[a]	.47[a]	.33[a]		.04	.22[a]	.53[a]	.22[a]	.46[a]	.28[a]
USA C_5	Religious Activity	.19[a]	.06[a]	.07[a]	.02	.09[a]	.05[b]		−.03	.10[a]	−.04	.08[a]	.06
C_6	Conflict with the Family	−.04	.11[a]	.07[a]	.11[a]	.13[a]	.05	.01		.14[a]	.14[a]	.29[a]	.20[a]
C_7	Educational Expectations	−.10[a]	.35[a]	.31[a]	.24[a]	.32[a]	.27[a]	.10[a]	.06[a]		.09[a]	.28[a]	.15[a]
X_1	School Social Climate (CLIME 1)	.08[a]	.17[a]	.13[a]	.15[a]	.33[a]	.26[a]	.09[a]	−.01	.21[a]		.40[a]	.39[a]
Z_1	Civics Knowledge	−.04	.35[a]	.31[a]	.29[a]	.71[a]	.37[a]	.08[a]	.13[a]	.40[a]	.43[a]		.51[a]
Y_1	Dissent Toleration	−.04	.21[a]	.20[a]	.20[a]	.38[a]	.22[a]	.02	.18[a]	.26[a]	.27[a]	.47[a]	

[a] Indicates significance level of .001 or better.
[b] Indicates significance level of .01 or better.

75

Knowledge and Civics Knowledge in both countries (.71 in the USA; .63 in the FRG). This is not surprising since doing well on the Civics Test requires that a student be able to understand a rather abstract vocabulary. The relationship between Word Knowledge and Type of Program is also strong, particularly in the Federal Republic of Germany. It is quite apparent from the matrix that stratification into different program types according to academic ability, student aspiration and family background is more pronounced in West Germany than in the United States. Moreover, the zero-order relationship between Type of Program and Dissent Toleration is stronger in the former country than in the latter. On the other hand, Dissent Toleration is more highly correlated with family status characteristics and Educational Expectations in the United States than in West Germany.

Since with the exception of Student Sex and Religious Activities, practically every variable is significantly correlated with every other, the independent relationships between variables can only be sorted out when more sophisticated statistical techniques are used. For this purpose, multiple regression analysis appeared to be the most appropriate.

Multiple Regression Analysis

The most rigorous test of the independent effects of a variable is a regression analysis in which all variables in the model are entered at once. Such an equation will show the strength of the relationship between a particular predictor variable and a criterion, controlling for all of the other variables in the model. The equation for such a model using Dissent Toleration as the criterion and all of the other variables as predictors is the following:

$$Y_1 = B_1C_1 + B_2C_2 + B_3C_3 + B_3C_3 + B_4C_4 + B_5C_5 + B_6X_1 + B_7Z_1 + E, \qquad (1)$$

where Y_1 is DISTOL 4D, B_1 through B_7 are standardized regression coefficients, C_1 through C_5 are conditioning variables (see Table 5.6), X_1 is the independent variable, School Social Climate, Z_1 is the intervening variable, Civics Knowledge, and E is the error term.

The Equation for the model in which Civics Knowledge is the criterion is as follows:

$$Z_1 = B_1C_1 + B_2C_2 + B_3C_3 + B_4C_4 + B_5C_5 + B_6X_1 + E, \qquad (2)$$

where the symbols have the same meanings as in equation (1).

Table 5.6 presents the results of the multiple regression analyses for Dissent Toleration and Civics Knowledge using both CLIME 1 and CLIME 3 as the social climate scales. Since Student Sex and Religious Activities were

Table 5.6 Standardized Regression Coefficients (Betas) for Multiple Regression Analysis of Dissent Toleration and Civics Knowledge -- USA and FRG

a. Using CLIME 1

Predictor	Dissent Toleration USA	FRG	Civics Knowledge USA	FRG
C_1 Parental SES	.036	.036	.064***	−.022
C_2 Word Knowledge	.068**	.053	.543***	.460***
C_3 Type of Program	.020	.015	.080***	.130***
C_4 Conflict w/Family	.133***	.036	.047***	.079**
C_5 Educational Expectations	.062**	−.016	.138***	.027
X_1 Social Climate (CLIME 1)	.087***	.210***	.189***	.190***
Z_1 Civics Knowledge	.321***	.378***	—	—
100 R^2	25.5	31.1	58.0	45.0
N	2167	933	2167	933

b. Using CLIME 3

Predictor	Dissent Toleration USA	FRG	Civics Knowledge USA	FRG
C_1 Parental SES	.045*	.045	.072***	−.018
C_2 Word Knowledge	.070***	.092***	.560***	.490***
C_3 Type of Program	.024	.022	.085***	.147***
C_4 Conflict w/Family	.133***	.049	.051***	.096***
C_5 Educational Expectations	.062**	−.026	.143***	.023
X_1 Social Climate (CLIME 3)	.071***	.075**	.154***	.147***
Z_1 Civics Knowledge	.332***	.415***	—	—
100 R^2	25.4	28.0	56.1	44.0
N	2475	1053	2368	987

NOTE: Significance levels of F tests indicated as follows: *** ≤ .001; ** ≤ .01; * ≤ .05.

eliminated from the analysis on the basis of their non-significant correlations with the criterion, the number of conditioning variables is reduced to five and they are renumbered.

Part "a" of Table 5.6 shows that in both countries many of the background factors disappear as predictors of Dissent Toleration in the presence of the other variables. Parental SES and Type of Program appear to have no independent effect on Dissent Toleration in the USA and the

FRG. The personal background variables Word Knowledge and Educational Expectations show slight independent effects (significant at the .01 level) for American 14-year-olds but not for the West Germans. What appears to be taking the greatest share of explained variance is the civics knowledge variable. The betas for this variable (.321 in USA; .378 in FRG) are by far the strongest ones in the model. The social climate variable in this analysis passes the test of significance, but is hardly a strong predictor of Dissent Toleration, especially in the USA. The results of the analysis are more encouraging for the Federal Republic in this respect (Beta = .21) when CLIME 1 is used, but as the "b" portion of the table shows, when CLIME 3 is used, Social Climate is reduced to the same position of weakness in that country, too.

It is notable that in the United States Conflict with the Family appears as the second strongest predictor of Dissent Toleration in the model. For the West German youth this variable is inconsequential. These results for the United States are somewhat difficult to interpret because of ambiguities in the question of causality. Two explanations appear possible. Either it could be said that youth who have grown up experiencing a certain amount of conflict in their families will be able to tolerate conflict in other arenas including the political one, or alternatively, youth who have been exposed to teachings and social contexts supportive of independence and nonconformity at school will tend to be more independent of (or in conflict with) their parents at home.

Table 5.6 also gives the results of the regression analysis for Civics Knowledge. It is interesting to note that the variables in the model explain a much greater percentage of the variance of this variable than of Dissent Toleration. This finding is to some extent a reflection of the substantially greater variance in Civics Knowledge compared to Dissent Toleration. But it is also to be expected since dissent toleration is a broad social norm that could be influenced by any number of the teenager's social experiences, while civics knowledge is a more specialized oucome influenced more by the specialized activities of the school and the student's capacity to learn.

The best measure of capacity to learn in the model, Word Knowledge, is clearly the most influential variable in predicting Civics Knowledge (Beta=.543 in USA; .400 in FRG). The next most important variable in both countries is Social Climate. Although the path to Dissent Toleration through strictly cognitive variables cannot be ignored, the indirect effect of Social Climate on Dissent Toleration still appears even when everything else is controlled.

Before leaving the regression analysis of Civics Knowledge, two important between-country differences should be noted. First, the education expectation variable is a significant predictor in the USA but not in the

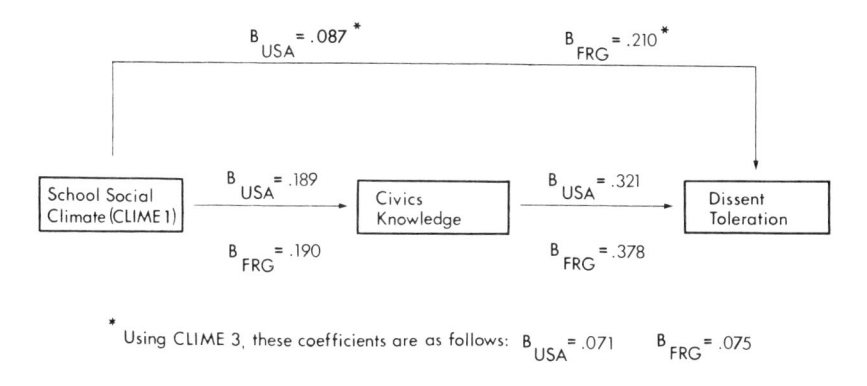

```
                    B_USA = .087 *                    B_FRG = .210 *
         ┌──────────────────────────────────────────────────────────────┐
         │                                                              ▼
┌─────────────────┐  B_USA = .189   ┌──────────┐  B_USA = .321   ┌──────────┐
│  School Social  │ ──────────────▶ │  Civics  │ ──────────────▶ │ Dissent  │
│ Climate (CLIME 1)│  B_FRG = .190  │Knowledge │  B_FRG = .378   │Toleration│
└─────────────────┘                 └──────────┘                 └──────────┘
```

* Using CLIME 3, these coefficients are as follows: $B_{USA} = .071$ $B_{FRG} = .075$

Figure 5.2. Relationships between School Social Climate, Civics Knowledge and Dissent Toleration Controlling for Conditioning Variables.

FRG. On the other hand, Type of Program is a significant predictor in the FRG, while its effect in the USA is nonsignificant. It seems that once a person has chosen an educational course in West Germany, his own future educational expectations are set. This impression is confirmed by the zero-order correlation of .53 between Type of Program and Educational Expectations. Thus, Educational Expectations have no relationship with learning outcomes independent of the Type of Program. In the USA, the type of program does not imply such a rigid differentiation with respect to future expectations. (The zero-order correlation between Type of Program and Educational Expectations in the USA is a moderate .27). In fact in the USA when expectations are in the model, the Type of Program maintains no independent relationship to Civics Knowledge.

Figure 5.2 summarizes the findings of the multiple regression analyses in terms of the original analytical model. The controls for the conditioning variables have been added and are reflected in the fact that the linkages between the variables are partial regression coefficients or beta weights (B). Although the strength of the linkages is reduced from those of the correlation analysis (Figure 5.1), all of the coefficients presented are significant at the .001 level except CLIME 3 with Dissent Toleration in the FRG, which is significant at the .01 level. In reference to the hypotheses of the study, the social climate of schooling does appear to be independently related to dissent toleration, both directly and indirectly through civics knowledge.

Contextual Analysis

In a previous section entitled "Unit of Analysis" the problem of "perceptual tendency" was discussed. The concept of perceptual tendency assumes that people perceive the same environmental stimuli differently, according to their own personal and background characteristics. Under this assumption, the relationship between social climate and dissent toleration may be explained, at least in part, by the fact that a single person responds to questions about both social phenomena in basically the same way.

As pointed out earlier, one way to design a test for perceptual tendency is to conduct a "contextual analysis." As McDill and Rigsby (1973) use the phrase, contextual analysis is an analysis in which some (or one) of the variables are measured at the group or aggregate level, while others, including the dependent variables, are measured at the individual level. Following the pattern set by Anderson (1970), the contextual analysis in this study measures school social climate at the group level, assigning each member in a school his school mean score, while all of the other variables are measured at the individual level.

If there were a perceptual tendency operating in this study one might expect a significant reduction in the relationship between social climate and dissent toleration when the contextual analysis is compared with the former regression analysis. This is because in the contextual analysis the social climate variable no longer represents a personal perception, but instead a consensus about the social climate, an external factor. The difference between the former regression analysis and the contextual analysis would give a rough indication of the magnitude of perceptual tendency. Moreover, by using the contextual analysis, perceptual tendency is removed as a source of explanation for the relationship between social climate and the outcome variables.

Table 5.7 presents the results of the contextual analysis. The main focus of this analysis is on the social climate variables, CLIME 1C (contextual) and CLIME 3C (contextual). A comparison between the aggregated and individual forms of these variables is facilitated by referring to Table 5.8.

Looking first at the analyses in which Dissent Toleration is the dependent variable, Table 5.8 shows that for the United States there is essentially no difference between the social climate variables in the contextual analysis and those in the non-contextual analysis. If anything, the strength of social climate as a predictor of dissent toleration is enhanced by the contextual analysis ($B_{CLIME\ 3}=.071$; $B_{CLIME\ 3C}=.082$). The analysis supports the interpretation that the relationship which exists between social climate and dissent toleration in the United States is not the result of a perceptual tendency within individuals.

The parallel analysis for the Federal Republic shows a decline in the predictive power of CLIME 1 in the contextual analysis, but not of CLIME 3. One interpretation of this finding is that it is the items in CLIME 1 which

Table 5.7 Standardized Regression Coefficients (Betas) for Multiple Regression Analysis of Dissent Toleration and Civics Knowledge using School Social Climate as a Contextual Variable -- USA and FRG

a. Using CLIME 1

Predictor	Dissent Toleration USA	FRG	Civics Knowledge USA	FRG
C_1 Parental SES	.043*	.047	.072***	−.014
C_2 Word Knowledge	.060**	.071*	.565***	.520***
C_3 Type of Program	.010	−.034	.081***	.122***
C_4 Conflict w/Family	.129***	.040	.037**	.086***
C_5 Educational Expectations	.062***	−.025	.149***	.015
W_1 Social Climate (Contextual) (CLIME 1C)	.084***	.140***	.106***	.037
Z_1 Civics Knowledge	.335***	.430***	—	—
100 R^2	25.6	29.0	56.0	42.0
N	3000	1316	3000	1316

b. Using CLIME 3

Predictor	Dissent Toleration USA	FRG	Civics Knowledge USA	FRG
C_1 Parental SES	.047*	.046	.078***	−.015
C_2 Word Knowledge	.060**	.086*	.569***	.531***
C_3 Type of Program	.013	.017	.088***	.133***
C_4 Conflict w/Family	.130***	.043	.038**	.086***
C_5 Educational Expectations	.061***	−.027	.149***	.012
W_1 Social Climate (Contextual) (CLIME 3C)[a]	.082***	.073*	.092***	−.028
Z_1 Civics Knowledge	.337***	.440***	—	—
100 R^2	25.6	28.0	55.8	42.0
N	3000	1316	3000	1316

NOTE: Significance levels of F tests indicated as follows: *** $\leq$ .001; ** $\leq$ .01; * $\leq$ .05.

[a] CLIME 3 in the contextual analysis for the USA differs from CLIME 3 in the individual level analysis on the Student Power item.

are not in CLIME 3 which are subject to perceptual tendency. These items are "Causes and explanations before names and dates," "Students agree with teacher," and "Every class member has same privileges." Further

Table 5.8   Partial Regression Coefficients for Contextual and Non-contextual Versions of Social Climate Scales

	Dependent Variable			
Social Climate Scale	Dissent Toleration USA	FRG	Civics Knowledge USA	FRG
CLIME 1	.087***	.210***	.189***	.190***
CLIME 1C (Contextual)	.084***	.140***	.106***	.037
CLIME 3	.071***	.075**	.154***	.147***
CLIME 3C (Contextual)	.082***	.073*	.092***	−.028

NOTE: Significance levels of F test indicated as follows: *** ⩽ .001; ** ⩽ .01; * ⩽ .05.

research is needed in order to determine whether or not this interpretation is valid and if so, why it occurs in West Germany but not in the United States.

The analyses in which Civics Knowledge is the dependent variable show a relative decline in the predictive power of the climate scales in the contextual analyses in both the USA and the FRG. In the analyses for the USA the regression coefficients are reduced in magnitude, but remain significant at the .001 level. In contrast, in the case of the FRG, the respective coefficients are reduced to statistical nonsignificance.

It would be difficult to interpret these results as evidence of perceptual tendency, since Civics Knowledge is not a measure of perceptions or attitudes, but an achievement test. What may be appearing instead is a case of differential perception of the environment according to the *performance characteristics* of the persons in the environment. In such a case those who achieved higher scores on the civics test would be those also more likely to perceive their school social climate in a positive light. If this interpretation is accurate, it is especially true in the case of the West German students.

The results of the contextual analysis may be summarized by referring to the above discussion and to Figure 5.3 below. There is no evidence that a perceptual tendency within individuals accounts for the relationship between School Social Climate and Dissent Toleration in the United States. There is evidence that perceptual tendency accounts for some of the relationship between the variables in West Germany when the "hand-picked" scale is used, but not when the factor analyzed scale is used.

The analyses give some indication that environment perception is related to the performance characteristics of the actors in the environment, i.e., that social climate perceptions of students are related to their achievement in

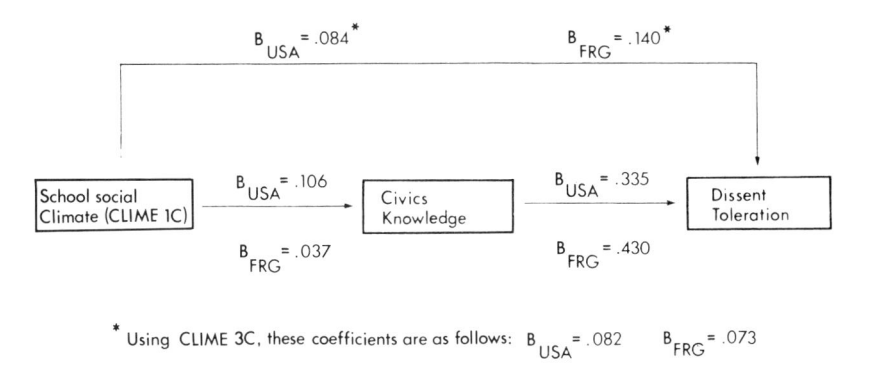

```
                    B_USA = .084*              B_FRG = .140*
          ┌─────────────────────────────────────────────────────┐
          │                                                     │
          │                                                     ▼
┌──────────────────┐  B_USA = .106  ┌──────────┐  B_USA = .335  ┌──────────┐
│ School social    │───────────────▶│ Civics   │───────────────▶│ Dissent  │
│ Climate (CLIME 1C)│  B_FRG = .037 │Knowledge │  B_FRG = .430  │Toleration│
└──────────────────┘                └──────────┘                └──────────┘
```

*Using CLIME 3C, these coefficients are as follows: $B_{USA} = .082$ $B_{FRG} = .073$

Figure 5.3. Relationships between School Social Climate, Civics Knowledge and Dissent Toleration in Contextual Analysis.

civics. The explanation does not completely account for the relationship between Social Climate and Civics Knowledge in the United States, but it nearly does so in the Federal Republic.

Disaggregating the Effects of School Social Climate

So far the school social climate dimensions have been analyzed together as a block. Since there are eight distinct dimensions of social climate, it is of theoretical and practical interest to see how each of the dimensions perform as independent predictors of dissent toleration and civics knowledge. Such an analysis was performed and the results are presented in Table 5.9.

In this analysis both dissent toleration and civics knowledge are treated as dependent variables. This is a departure from the regular analytical model in which Civics Knowledge is treated as an intervening variable and is thus entered as a control when Dissent Toleration is the criterion. The interest in this analysis is not so much in testing a model as in showing the relative strength of the relationships between separate social climate dimensions and cognitive and affective outcomes. However, as with the former regression analyses, the conditioning variables are entered as controls. The social climate variables used in this analysis are those from the scale, CLIME 1.

Looking at the results for the United States, it appears that "Causes and explanations before names and dates" is the strongest independent social climate predictor of Dissent Toleration. It is followed by "Students bring up current events," Peer Group Interaction, Ritual Climate, and Independence of Thought, in that order. Although statistically significant, the last four

Table 5.9 Standardized Regression Coefficients for the Regression of Social Climate Dimensions on Dissent Toleration and Civics Knowledge[a]

Social Climate Variable	Dissent Toleration USA	FRG	Civics Knowledge USA	FRG
Every class member has same privileges	.041*	.080**	.054***	−.090***
Peer Group Interaction Scale	.073***	.089**	.106***	.129***
Independence of Thought Scale	.058***	.161***	.042**	.106***
Causes and explanations before names and dates	.113***	.208***	.101***	.183***
Students bring up current events	.081***	.051	.080***	−.047
Ritual Climate Scale	−.068***	−.138***	−.051***	−.142***
Students agree with teacher	.037*	.102***	.091***	.097***
Students make school policies	.021	.051	.049***	−.013
N	~2750[b]	~1200[b]	~2500[b]	~1200[b]

NOTE: Significance levels of F test indicated as follows: *** ≤ .001; ** ≤ .01; * ≤ .05.

[a] The conditioning variables controlled are: Parental SES, Word Knowledge, Type of Program, Conflict w/Family and Educational Expectations.

[b] The exact number of cases used in each calculation varied since the numbers of missing cases were different for each variable.

are rather weak independent predictors in terms of the amount of the total variance they explain (2%).

In the FRG, the relative ordering of the social climate predictors of Dissent Toleration is quite different. "Causes and explanations" is the strongest predictor in that country also, followed this time by Independence of Thought, Ritual Climate, "Students agree with teacher," and Peer Group Interaction. Generally speaking, the Beta coefficients are higher for the FRG than for the USA, although with the exception of the one for "Causes and explanations...," the magnitude of the coefficients is rather low.

In Figure 5.4 the regression coefficients are plotted in a way that shows the strength of each social climate dimension relative to the other dimensions in the same country and to the same dimension in the other country. In both countries, dissent toleration appears to flourish best in schools which deemphasize "rote and ritual,"[4] i.e., learning names and dates and

---
[4] This phrase is utilized by Schwille (1975) to describe IEA civics outcomes.

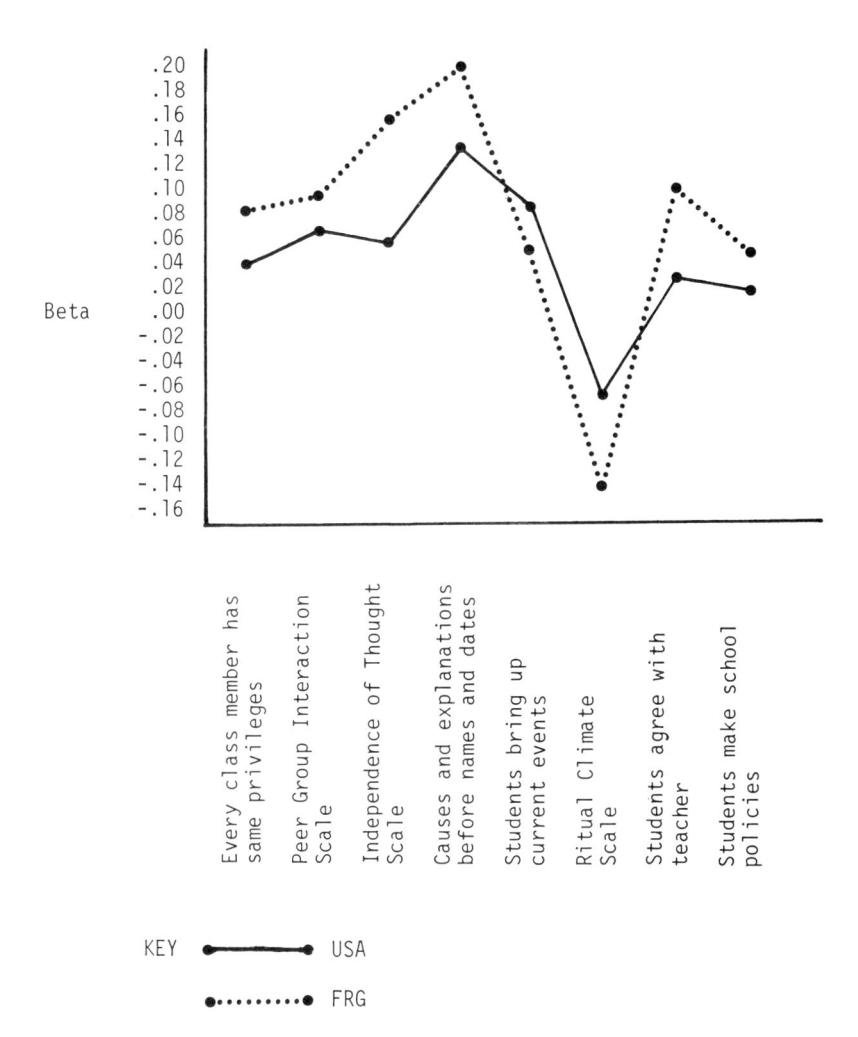

Figure 5.4. Standardized Regression Coefficients for the Relationships between Social Climate Variables and Dissent Toleration Controlling for Conditioning Variables—USA and FRG.

engaging in patriotic rituals. In addition, in West Germany student independence, as measured both by amount of disagreement with the teacher in the classroom and by perceived encouragement towards independent thought, is more characteristic of schools promoting dissent toleration. In the United States on the other hand, political action, as measured by student initiative in discussing current events and the tendency to rely on voting for decision making in peer groups, has a relatively stronger impact on dissent norms.

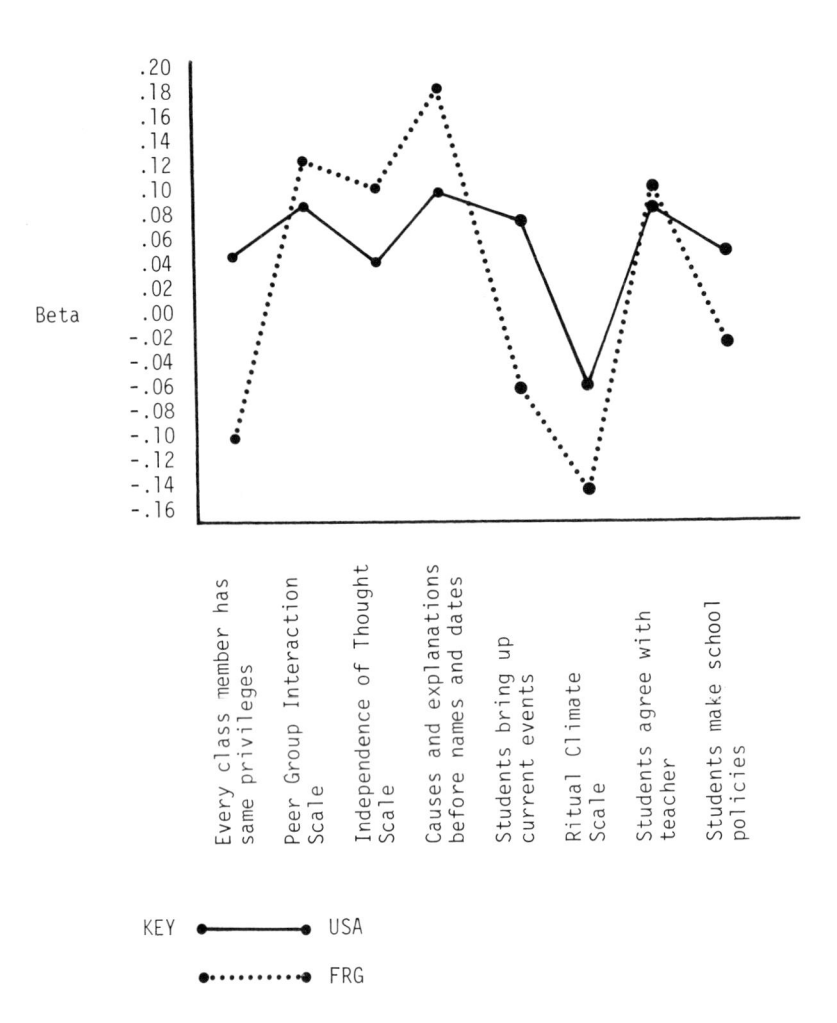

Figure 5.5. Standardized Regression Coefficients for the Relationships between Social Climate Variables and Civics Knowledge controlling for Conditioning Variables—USA and FRG.

When Civics Knowledge is the criterion, the analysis yields essentially the same findings as above. Figure 5.5 shows the results in graphic form. Rote and ritual are negatively related to civics cognitive achievement in both countries. Student independence is also important in both countries, though somewhat more so in the FRG. A surprising outcome in analysis for the Federal Republic is the finding that the classroom equality, political environment, and student power variables are negatively related to civics cognitive achievement. This suggests that in West German schools lower achievement is related to student political activism and the equalization of the classroom reward structure. Since the coefficients for the predictors in question are relatively weak, however, this interpretation is at best tentative, and should be tested in greater depth.

In a previous section in this chapter it was suggested that Peer Group Interaction and "Students agree with teacher" were not variables likely to *influence* civics knowledge. It was suggested that these factors might be associated with academic ability, which is what is really influencing civics learning. In the present analysis, the academic ability measure, Word Knowledge, is statistically controlled. Even so, Peer Group Interaction and "Students agree with teacher" are still related to Civics Knowledge at significance levels greater than .001 in both countries. Thus the relationship is independent of academic ability.

This still does not establish the fact that the above climate items *influence* civics achievement. As the preceding section indicated, Civics Knowledge could be viewed as a performance characteristic which influences the student's perception of his environment. Those who achieve high scores in civics may well perceive more conflict with teachers and be more inclined to report the use of democratic procedures in their peer group interactions. They may also perceive less classroom equality and participation, which could account for the negative coefficients found in Table 5.9.

Regression Analysis by Type of Program for the Federal Republic of Germany

The findings already discussed indicate that the type of program variable has special significance in the Federal Republic of Germany. To a greater extent in that country than in the USA, zero-order correlations revealed strong relationships between Type of Program and other variables in the model. One of the regression analyses reported in Table 5.6 showed it to be a significant independent predictor of Civics Knowledge. Another multiple regression analysis not reported on in the tables included an interaction vector between Social Climate and Type of Program. As a predictor this vector was found to be statistically significant (at the .001 level) in the Federal Republic and not in the United States. Such a finding gave birth to the notion that school social climate might be having different effects on dissent toleration depending upon the type of school being considered. This notion prompted the investigator to conduct separate multiple regression analyses within each program type. The results of these analyses are reported in Table 5.10.

The table shows clearly that the climate variable does in fact have different impacts on Dissent Toleration depending on the type of program.

Table 5.10 Dissent Toleration Regression Analysis by Type of Program -- FRG

Predictor	Hauptschule Mean	Beta	Realschule Mean	Beta	Gymnasium Mean	Beta
Parental SES	---[a]	.028	---[a]	-.015	---[a]	.058
Word Knowledge	9.73	.002	19.52	.190**	25.16	.039
Educational Expectations	2.04	-.028	2.57	.088	3.75	-.020
Conflict w/ Family	1.50	-.030	1.67	.106	1.76	.165
Social Climate (CLIME 1)[b]	21.76	.294***	23.06	.050	22.50	.106
Civics Knowledge	22.87	.360***	30.12	.290***	33.13	.275***
100 R^2		29.7		22.8		14.3
N		532		232		167
Mean DISTOL 4D Score	.663		.776		.802	

NOTE: Significance levels of F tests indicated as follows: *** ≤ .001; ** ≤ .01; * ≤ .05.

[a] SES was constructed like a standard score such that the mean was always zero. An indicator of parent status differences is the Father's occupation. On a scale from 1 to 3 the mean scores by school type for this variable are as follows: Hauptschule, 1.88; Realschule, 2.08; Gymnasium, 2.42.

[b] Scores reported here are non-standardized.

The independent effect of Social Climate on Dissent Toleration is considerably stronger in the *Hauptschule* than in the other two programs. In fact, it is only in the *Hauptschule* that social climate is a statistically significant predictor. The fact that over 50% of the sample is drawn from this type of program is presumably what makes social climate appear to be a significant predictor for the full sample.

The results of the regression analysis for the *Realschule* are difficult to interpret. The only significant predictors at this level are the cognitive ones, Word Knowledge and Civics Knowledge. This is the only analysis in which Word Knowledge remains significant as a predictor even in the presence of Civics Knowledge. It is known that scholastic aptitude is important in determining whether a student will stay in the lowest track (*Hauptschule*) or move on to a higher one. The mean scores for Word Knowledge and Civics

Knowledge are considerably higher for *Realschule* students than for *Hauptschule* students. It may be that the superior ability of the *Realschule* students is what determines their attitudes on a whole range of issues. It is also possible that a variable not in the model is taking the place of social climate in the *Realschule* analysis. In this case variance not accounted for by social climate would appear in the error term (E) in the model. The table shows that in fact the error term is larger for the *Realschule* analysis than for the *Hauptschule* analysis. Seven percent less of the variance is explained by the variables in the model in the former analysis than in the latter.

The model explains even less of the variance for *Gymnasium* students (14.3% as opposed to 29.7% for *Hauptschule* students). This is in part accounted for by the fact that their mean score on Dissent Toleration is so high (.80) and their standard deviation on the same so low (.15). In short, there is less variance to explain. Cognitive Civics is still a relatively strong predictor at the *Gymnasium* level. Second most important at this level is Conflict with the Family. The social climate variable is stronger at this level than at the *Realschule* level, but it is not statistically significant.

It is tempting to conclude that some variable or set of variables such as the school "charter" is influencing political attitudes more at the *Gymnasium* level. The school "charter" concept (Meyer, 1970) is based on the assertion that students of elite schools are aware of their status and so more or less automatically assume the values of elite adults, independent of any socializing influences which may be present in social agencies such as the school. This theory may partially account for the higher levels of dissent toleration in the elite *Gymnasium* and the low percentage of variance explained by the model. This explanation receives additional support in the research conducted by Weiler (1971, pp. 28–33). Further research in which the concept of "charter" is carefully operationalized is needed in order to unambiguously affirm this hypothesis.

Path Analyses

Up to this point the results of the study have been discussed in terms of *relationships* between variables and not in terms of *effects* or *causal* outcomes. One method for testing hypotheses concerning the causal ordering of variables is path analysis (Blalock, 1964, 1969, 1971; Duncan, 1966, 1969; Boudon, 1968). According to this method, causal inferences can be drawn by the researchers by testing hypotheses formulated on the basis of theoretical considerations (Kerlinger and Pedhazur, 1973, p. 305). The variables in the model are ordered according to what is assumed to be the best causal "priority" and then the assumptions are tested using multiple regression techniques. At each stage of the causal sequence a particular variable becomes the dependent variable; the variables to its left (when the variables are order from left to right) become its predictors or determinants. Standardized regression coefficients at each stage are what are referred to as the "path coefficients."

Figure 5.6 presents the form of the path model referred to as the "Basic Path Model" for both countries. It is so named because the variables in it are the strongest and theoretically most important in the study. The social climate scale used in these analyses is CLIME 3, the factor analyzed scale. Instead of using a single exogenous variable, Parental SES, the family background measure has been broken down into its constituent parts, Father's Education, Mother's Education and Father's Occupation. Residuals are given in their nonreduced forms so that the percentage of the variance explained by the model (R^2) at each step can be seen. Only path coefficients that are stronger than .100 are included in the diagrams. According to standards commonly applied, these are the paths which are of at least moderate strength.[5]

Consider the Basic Path Model for the United States first. Father's Education and Father's Occupation are both moderately strong predictors of Word Knowledge. Of the two, Father's Education is slightly stronger. Word Knowledge is a strong predictor of Type of Program and Civics Knowledge. The causal relationship between Word Knowledge and Civics Knowledge is by far the strongest in the model. Word Knowledge is also a moderately strong predictor of School Social Climate.

At the next step, Type of Program is shown to be a moderately strong predictor of School Social Climate. In addition, Type of Program and Social Climate are both found to have moderate direct effects on Civics Knowledge. The latter relationship appears to confirm one of the major hypotheses of the study, the one highlighting the indirect relationship between school social climate and dissent toleration. The balance of the confirmation comes at the next step in the model, where Civics Knowledge is found to be a strong predictor of Dissent Toleration in the USA.

In short, the basic path analysis reveals the predominance of cognitive paths to Dissent Toleration. Father's Education affects the student's ability to learn facts and information about civic affairs which then affects his ability to tolerate political conflict. However, the paths through Type of Program and Social Climate cannot be ignored. Students with better verbal skills are selected into the more advanced school tracks where the learning climates appear to be more conducive to high achievement on the civics

---

[5] The following expressions are often used in judging the strength of path coefficients: Less than .05, not important; .05–.100, weak; .101–.250, moderate; greater than .251, strong. (Fägerlind, 1975)

Figure 5.6. Basic Path Model—USA and FRG.

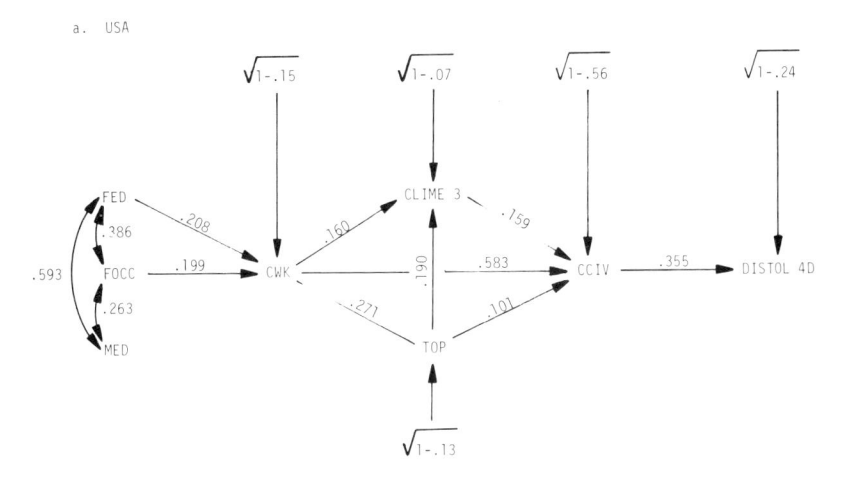

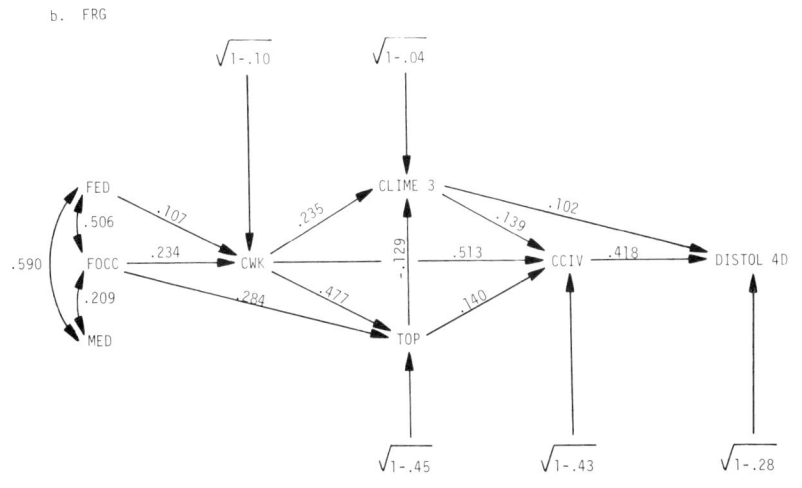

a. USA

b. FRG

Key to acronyms: FED = Father's Education; MED = Mother's Education; FOCC = Father's Occupation; CWK = Word Knowledge (Corrected); CLIME 3 = School Social Climate Scale; TOP = Type of Program; CCIV = Civics Knowledge (Corrected); DISTOL 4D = Dissent Toleration Scale.

test. The learning climate is also directly related to Dissent Toleration, but the relationship is too weak (.071) to be represented in the diagram.

The Basic Path Model for the Federal Republic (Figure 5.6b) reveals essentially the same relationships, but with some interesting differences. The cognitive paths predominate in this country's model also. However, in the FRG Father's Occupation is a much stronger predictor of Word Knowledge than is Father's Education (the stronger predictor in the USA).

91

In addition, there is a strong direct relationship between Father's Occupation and Type of Program, a relationship which gives important insights into the social stratification processes of the West German school system.[6] Type of Program is also strongly related to Word Knowledge (much more so in the FRG than in the USA), giving further evidence of a stratification process.

Another interesting contrast involves the path between Type of Program and School Social Climate. Surprisingly, the path coefficient indicates a negative relationship (B= —.129). This is particularly surprising since the simple correlation between the two variables is a negligible .03. Two possible explanations will be advanced in an attempt to account for this phenomenon.

The first is a methodological explanation, involving the problem of multicollinearity. This problem often arises in multiple regression analyses when independent variables are highly intercorrelated (Gordon, 1968). In this case, two predictors of Social Climate, Type of Program and Word Knowledge, are correlated with a coefficient of .59. Normally multicollinearity is not considered a serious problem unless the simple correlation is around .80. Nevertheless, the problem may be present in this analysis to some extent, which means that once Word Knowledge is taken into account, it is difficult to determine what the independent effect of the correlate, Type of Program, really is. The negative sign on the path coefficient may thus be a statistical artifact.

However, there may be another way to account for the finding. It assumes that multicollinearity is not a problem. It also assumes the type of academic program one attends in West Germany is a function of both academic ability (for which Word Knowledge is a proxy) and a set of other variables including motivation, aspirations, self-image, status, and so forth. It is possible that the part of Type of Program not accounted for by academic ability *is* actually negatively related to social climate perception. For example, concentrating on one variable suggested above, status, it is possible that those of higher status tend to view their social climate with a more critical eye. This is consistent with findings of Torney, Oppenheim and Farnen (1975), who indicate that high status students in West Germany tend to view social institutions in general with a substantial amount of cynicism.

Unfortunately, it was not within the scope of this study to pursue this question in greater depth. This must await further analyses.

The West German Basic Model also differs from that of the United

---

[6] More will be said about this in the next chapter.

Figure 5.7. Expanded Path Model—USA and FRG.

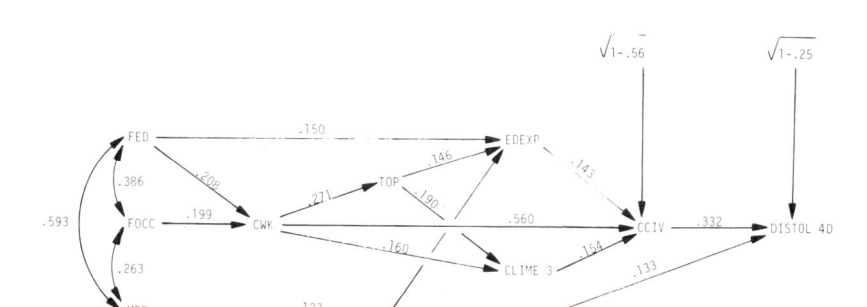

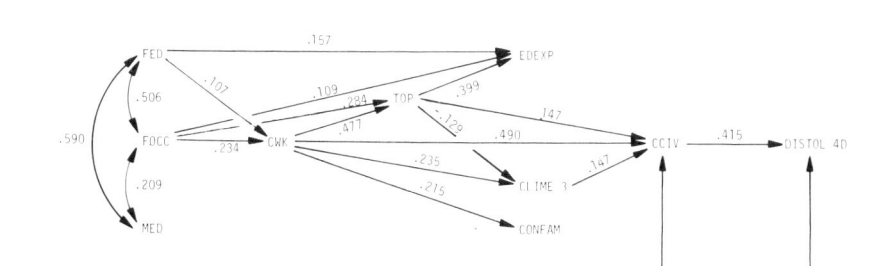

a. USA

b. FRG

Key to acronyms: FED = Father's Education; MED = Mother's Education; FOCC = Father's Occupation; CWK = Word Knowledge (Corrected); CLIME 3 = School Social Climate Scale; TOP = Type of Program; CCIV = Civics Knowledge (Corrected); DISTOL 4D = Dissent Toleration Scale.

States in the paths between School Social Climate and the variables for which it is a predictor, Dissent Toleration and Civics Knowledge. Figure 5.6b indicates that there is a moderate direct path between CLIME 3 and DISTOL 4D in the Federal Republic. The magnitude of the path coefficient linking CLIME 3 and Civics Knowledge (CCIV) is not significantly different from that in the model for the USA. However, the findings of the contextual analysis remain to challenge the meaningfulness of these linkages. These findings were not incorporated into the path analysis. If they had been, the paths between CLIME 3 and CCIV would have been reduced in strength in both countries, but in the FRG to the point of statistical nonsignificance. Thus, although the path diagrams indicate the existence of moderately strong paths between Social Climate and Civics Knowledge, this finding may be (especially for the FRG) a reflection of the tendency of high achieving students to rate their classrooms more positively.

Figure 5.7 presents the diagram for an Expanded Path Model for both countries. This model is called expanded because two additional conditioning variables are added, Educational Expectations (EDEXP) and Conflict with the Family (CONFAM). In the theoretical model, CONFAM is treated as a concurrent condition and EDEXP as an anticipatory one. Although this distinction is conceptually interesting, it was not possible to place them in different locations in the analytical model. Thus, in the expanded path model, they are both entered as if they were concurrent with School Social Climate.

The Expanded Model adds some additional explanatory power to the model for the United States. There are moderately strong linkages between Educational Expectations and Civics Knowledge, and between Conflict with the Family and Dissent Toleration. There are also several paths leading to Educational Expectations in the model including Mother's Education, which has not entered the model in either country until this point. In contrast, there were no significant paths leading to Conflict with the Family in the model. With the additional controls entered, the expanded model explains slightly more (1%) of the variance in Dissent Toleration.

Expanding the model for the Federal Republic adds nothing to the amount of variance explained in the dependent variable, Dissent Toleration. Father's Status and Type of Program help to determine Educational Expectations, but EDEXP has no significant independent impact on cognitive or attitudinal outcomes. CONFAM is affected by Word Knowledge (smarter students seem to disagree more with their elders), but it does not affect the criteria. Thus EDEXP and CONFAM are essentially "dead-end" variables in the West German model. All of the impacts upon Civics Knowledge and Dissent Toleration in this country are through either cognitive or school quality variables.

Summary of Results

This chapter has reported on several different kinds of analyses. First was a univariate analysis which showed (among other things) that West German youth scored higher on the measure of dissent toleration than did the youth from the United States (or any other IEA country). Although the American youth did not score as high as the West German youth, they did appear to be more tolerant of dissent than their compatriots of a decade ago.

Further analyses revealed that there were substantial zero-order correlations between many of the variables in the study. However, two variables, Student Sex and Religious Activity, were eliminated from the research model on the basis of their non-significant correlations with Dissent Toleration. All other variables entered into various waves of a multiple regression analysis. Each successive wave of the analysis was a more stringent test of the hypothesis that the social climate of schooling was positively related to dissent toleration both directly and indirectly through the intervening variable, civics knowledge. In the first wave, using the hand-picked climate scale, CLIME 1, the hypotheses received solid support, all of the relevant regression coefficients in both countries being significant at the .001 level or better. In the next wave, the factor analyzed scale, CLIME 3, was used. Here, too, the hypotheses were both confirmed in both countries, although the strength of the relationships between social climate and the outcome variables was reduced, especially in the case of the Federal Republic. In the final wave of the analysis, the social climate measures were treated as contextual variables to correct for a possible "perceptual tendency." Under these rigorous conditions, with all conditioning variables in the model, using the factor analyzed climate scale and correcting for "perceptual tendency," all but one of the hypotheses were again upheld. The one hypothesis that was rejected was the one for indirect links between social climate and dissent toleration in the Federal Republic, since the link between social climate and civics knowledge was found to be statistically nonsignificant. An explanation was offered for the disappearance of the relationship under these conditions.

The next set of analyses considered the independent relationships of individual school climate dimensions to dissent toleration and civics knowledge. In both countries dissent toleration and civics learning appear to flourish best in schools which deemphasize "rote and ritual." In addition, in the Federal Republic the two outcome variables are correlated with climate dimensions relating to student independence. In contrast, in the United States the outcomes are more strongly tied to measures of student political activity.

Following up on evidence of interactions between type of program and social climate in predicting dissent toleration in the Federal Republic, a separate regression analysis was conducted within each school type for that country. The finding was that social climate was a relatively strong predictor of dissent toleration in the *Hauptschule* only. Possible explanations were offered for why this was not the case in the *Realschule* and the *Gymnasium*.

Finally, the results of some exercises in path modelling were presented. A Basic Path Model was first examined, which contained the most important variables in the study. All of the "strong" paths but one in the models involved cognitive variables, Word Knowledge or Civics Knowledge, either as predictors or outcomes. The one exception was the path between Father's Occupation and Type of Program in the FRG, suggesting the existence of educational stratification according to family background. In addition, there were moderate paths through School Social Climate to Civics

Knowledge in both countries and to Dissent Toleration in the Federal Republic, although the directionality of some of these paths was uncertain, given the results of the contextual analysis.

The Expanded Path Model entered Educational Expectations and Conflict with the Family as additional predictors at the level of School Social Climate. In the case of the United States the two additional variables added to the explanatory power of the model. In the West German model the two variables led to "dead ends," i.e., they were affected by variables in the model but did not themselves have a significant independent impact on any.

The findings reported above reveal interesting similarities and differences in the socialization processes involving 14-year-olds in the United States and West Germany. Along the way some interpretive remarks have been ventured. In the next and final chapter, the findings will be considered separately for each country and put back into the broader social perspective presented in the first chapter.

Chapter 6
Summary and Conclusions

One of the most highly cherished values of the liberal democratic system of government is its guarantee of civil liberties: freedom of speech, freedom of association, and freedom from arbitrary arrest and detention. Although these freedoms are guaranteed in theory in all Western democracies, in practice they are often violated in all. Reasons for this discrepancy abound, both at the systemic and at the individual levels. At the systemic level, the machinery of government, its political institutions, may not be adequately developed to cope with all the conflicts and pressures which inevitably accompany the practice of civil liberties. At the individual level, citizens may not be sufficiently informed or sufficiently tolerant to allow others to speak out against things they value highly. One of the great ironies of democratic politics is that people so often deny to others the values which they hold sacred for themselves, namely freedom of expression and association.

Individual tolerance of conflicting political points of view ("dissent toleration") is the main focus of the present study. Dissent toleration is considered to be an important aspect of "ideological democratic commitment." As an individual value, it can be influenced over time by socializing agents such as the family, the school and the work place. Early childhood experiences are important, since they shape general perceptions and self-concepts which relate to tolerance. However, the teen-age years are also important, since it is during adolescence that people begin to understand abstract political concepts and formulate manifestly political positions. In addition, it is at this point in life that schools and peer groups appear to exert a considerable influence on a person's political attitudes and values.

Evidence was presented in Chapter 1 which showed that political tolerance was a value which was clearly related to a person's educational level. Less clear, however, has been our understanding of what aspects of education influence such values and by what processes. In order to answer these questions, some analysts have focused on the school curriculum as the key. Others have emphasized teacher characteristics, the social milieu or the organizational structure of schooling. Still others have singled out the process of status allocation and its consequences.

This study was designed to test an analytical model relating dissent toleration to two aspects of the educational process: 1) the school's social climate, and 2) the student's acquired knowledge of democratic principles and institutions (civics knowledge). It was hypothesized that the school social climate would influence dissent toleration *directly* through such processes as generalization and interpersonal transference and *indirectly* through its impact on civics knowledge. As an intervening variable, civics knowledge was assumed to relate to dissent toleration by making students more aware of the importance of civil liberties and more informed about dissenting groups.

The above hypotheses were tested among secondary school youth in two national settings, the United States of America and the Federal Republic of Germany. The data from these countries were gathered by the International Association for the Evaluation of Educational Achievement (IEA) in 1971. For the United States, a national sample of over 3,000 14-year-olds was available for analysis. For the Federal Republic, a sample representing ten of eleven states and over 1,300 14-year-olds was available. These particular countries were chosen partly because of the salience of the issue of dissent toleration in them and partly because they were both highly industrialized countries with well-developed and relatively stable political institutions.

The present investigation treats the analyses in the two countries as replications of one another. The aim was not to explain absolute differences in achievement and attitudes between countries, but to compare processes and models. In doing so, a number of outcomes were found to be generalizable to both national contexts. Other findings were more idiosyncratic. This chapter will first summarize the findings which applied to youth in both countries. Then it will treat each country separately, summarizing the findings which applied in only one national setting. After these summaries, it will dwell on some of the policy implications of this research. Finally, it will propose some suggestions for further research.

General Findings

1. Following Moos' conceptualization of social climate, it was possible to construct from IEA data school social climate measures which were reasonably strong correlates of student performance and attitudes. Since this study was a secondary analysis (i.e., used data collected by other researchers), the creation of social climate scales provided a special challenge. Many of the items chosen for the scale had never been used together before. In addition, some items represented a student's point of view, and others an administrator's. Had the author been able to design a coherent social climate scale from the beginning (i.e., prior to data collection), it is probable that the correlations produced would have been stronger than those reported in the current study.

2. School Social Climate appeared as a significant predictor of Dissent Toleration, even when rigorous statistical tests were applied, including controls for five conditioning variables and one intervening variable, the use of

a factor analyzed climate scale and correction for perceptual tendency. However, the fact that the partial regression coefficients were significant does not mean that they were particularly strong. In fact, with all of the controls present, School Social Climate explained no more than 4% of the variance in Dissent Toleration.

3. In most analyses, Civics Knowledge acted as a mediator between School Social Climate and Dissent Toleration, as was predicted by the analytical model. The links between Civics Knowledge and Dissent Toleration were especially strong in both countries. However, the results of the contextual analysis indicated that the links between Social Climate and Civics Knowledge may not have been as strong as they originally appeared. This was especially the case in the FRG and will be discussed in greater depth under item 8 for that country.

4. School Social Climate was more highly correlated with Civics Knowledge than with Dissent Toleration. This is consistent with other studies based on IEA data, in which school quality variables generally explained more of the variance of specific school subjects (math, science, or French) than of more general skills (verbal ability) or attitudes (anti-authoritarianism). Compared with the specific school subjects, such general skills and attitudes are much more likely to be influenced by the home environment, peer group pressures or mass media exposure.

5. Two of the strongest social climate dimensions in predicting Civics Knowledge and Dissent Toleration were Cognitive Climate ("Causes and explanations before names and dates") and Ritual Climate (which was negatively related to the criteria). Similar findings were reported by Schwille (1975) who called this the "negative relationship of rote and ritual" to achievement in civic education (pp. 149–153).

6. No statistical relationship between Student Sex and either Dissent Toleration or Civics Knowledge was found. Likewise, there was no relationship between Religious Activity and the two learning outcomes. The latter finding disconfirmed the expectation that religious activity and dissent toleration would be negatively correlated.

7. Parental Socioeconomic Status was not found to be directly related to Dissent Toleration or Civics Knowledge when the other variables in the model were controlled. With few exceptions, the path model seemed to fit the resource conversion theory conceived by Coleman (1971) and refined by Fägerlind (1975). According to this theory, family resources are converted into personal resources which are then converted into different socialization settings and further personal resources. In the present model,

parental SES is converted into student verbal ability (Word Knowledge) which influences the type of program the student enters and the type of social climate he will be exposed to. These, in conjunction with the verbal ability measure, determine the student's achievement in civics (another personal resource). This resource then becomes a strong predictor of the final outcome, dissent toleration. A rather glaring exception to this pattern is found in the West German model and is discussed under point 4 for that country.

8. There was little evidence in this study for the existence of a "perceptual tendency" in the students' responses to the social climate and dissent toleration items. This means that students did not automatically answer questions about social climate and dissent in the same manner. This is consistent with the findings of Stern (1964), Walberg and Anderson (1968) and Moos and Bromet (1976), who, in separate analyses, determined that environment perceptions did not depend on individual background or personality characteristics. There was, however, some indication that social climate perception was related to a student's performance characteristics in the particular setting, the higher achieving students perceiving their learning environments more positively. This is also consistent with Moos and Bromet (1976).

9. Although the analytical technique of path analysis lends credibility to the notion that higher levels of dissent toleration and civics knowledge are in part a consequence of the social climate of schooling, it is also possible to order the variables in the other direction, social climate perception being a consequence of the other two variables. Since IEA was not able to randomly assign students to different social climate types (or even to conduct some form of pretesting), one cannot rule out the possibility that some students selected particular kinds of classrooms because of their records of high achievement or because they were more tolerant in the first place.

However, there are a number of ways to challenge this selection hypothesis as an explanation of the results of this study. First, it is not clear how free students really were to choose their own classes. Many schools, at least in the United States, required certain courses for which there were only one or two teachers. Often students were assigned to one class or another according to rather arbitrary criteria.

Second, if students were assigned according to a tracking system, better students being assigned to higher level classes with better climates for learning, then the research model had a control for selection effects already built in: the variable, Type of Program. Social Climate was shown to be related to Civics Knowledge even after Type of Program was controlled.

Third, since the sampling units were students and schools and not classrooms, it is hard to talk about selection into individual classrooms. Random samples of students were drawn from the schools and asked to comment on their civics classes in general. One climate dimension was not even based on the student questionnaire, but on an administrator's response to a school questionnaire. Therefore, the study refers to school social climate, not classroom social climate. Students were even less likely to have had the option of choosing the school whose climate they preferred than that of choosing a preferred classroom.

Although not conclusive, these arguments do make the selection hypothesis appear less plausible.

Specific Findings for the United States

1. Using the results from a particular Dissent Toleration item ("Newspapers should be allowed to print anything...") as an indicator, the American students sampled by IEA appeared to be considerably more tolerant of dissent than those surveyed eleven years earlier by Remmers (1963). The significance of this finding changes somewhat when put in international perspective. While American youth of the early 1970's appeared more tolerant than those of the previous decade, they were, on the average, less tolerant than those from three of eight IEA nations.

2. The analytical model explained a lower proportion of the variance in Dissent Toleration in the United States than in West Germany (24% as compared with 28%). This could be a result of the greater impact of factors like peer groups and mass media in the United States. Unfortunately, there were not enough good indicators of such constructs in the IEA data to represent them adequately in the analytical model.

3. Conflict with the Family was a more important predictor of Dissent Toleration in the United States than in the Federal Republic of Germany.

4. Educational Expectations was a more important predictor of Civics Knowledge in the United States than in the Federal Republic. This could reflect the lower emphasis placed on ability grouping in the former country compared with the latter. After students in West Germany are placed in various schools, their educational expectations are more or less fixed. Thus, Educational Expectations adds no explanatory power to the model in that country after Type of Program is partialled out.

5. There was a positive relationship between Type of Program and School Social Climate in the United States. This indicates that students in the higher status programs (i.e., college-bound) perceived their learning environments as more open and tolerant. It is quite likely, since better teachers

are generally assigned to such programs, that such perceptions were a reflection of an external reality.

6. Mother's Education appeared in the United States model as an independent predictor of Educational Expectations. Even with the paternal background variables controlled, mother's education influenced the child's educational expectations. This finding is consistent with the literature in the United States concerning maternal education and child aspirations (Sewell and Shah, 1968). It is interesting to note that in West-Germany, Mother's Education was not independently related to any of the variables in the research model. It is also interesting that in the USA, Mother's Education was not independently related to any other variable in the model, including Word Knowledge, as might have been expected.

7. While Dissent Toleration was negatively related to "rote and ritual" in both countries, in the United States it was positively related to social climate dimensions indicating student political activity. A plausible explanation for this might be that students who were more politically active in school attained higher levels of "internal control" or "subjective competence" (Wittes, 1972; Almond and Verba, 1963). Students who feel competent and in control of their lives would generally feel less threatened by the challenge of political dissenters. Indeed, such students are more likely to be dissenters or future dissenters themselves.

Specific Findings for the Federal Republic

1. West German 14-year-olds were by far the most tolerant national group of any in the IEA survey. This finding sheds new light on the Dahrendorf contention (1967) that the "liberal" political conception "has never really gained a hold in Germany." Perhaps the educational change that Dahrendorf himself helped to shape had begun to bear liberal fruit in teenagers of the early 1970's.

2. The above interpretation could be challenged in the light of the high refusal rate in the West German sample. It is possible that those schools which were capable of returning high scores on the tests were more likely to participate in the study. However, in light of the politicization of the schools in the early 1970's in West Germany, it is equally possible that the high performance schools were so caught up in internal struggles and self-assessment that they decided not to be bothered by yet another survey. Unfortunately, the IEA country report from the Federal Republic does not present evidence favoring one interpretation or the other.

3. The analytical model of this study explains a higher proportion of the variance in Dissent Toleration in the Federal Republic than in the United States. Perhaps teachers and parents no longer believe (as they formerly did, according to Kob, 1963) that the school should have a marginal impact on student attitudes and values. The school impacts found in this study appear to be quite substantial, especially at the level of the *Hauptschule*.

4. Student ability and family background factors appeared as significant predictors of the type of program (school) attended by West German students. Since the school types occupy distinct status positions in West German society, this phenomenon could be referred to as educational stratification by ability and family background. Father's Occupation appears as the strongest family background stratifier in the model. The direct relationship between Father's Occupation and Type of Program is one that does not fit the resource conversion theory, but suggests a stratification theory as more appropriate.[1]

5. Type of Program was a more powerful variable in the West German analysis than in the analysis for the United States. When it was in the model, Educational Expectations had no impact on Civics Knowledge. This seems to indicate that once the school type has been determined, educational expectations are also set. Also, an interaction between Type of Program and Social Climate appeared, such that climate was more important as a predictor of Dissent Toleration in one school type (*Hauptschule*) than in the others. Finally, there was a negative coefficient for the path between Type of Program and Social Climate in the West German model. This could either be the consequence of multicollinearity (see Chapter 5) or a reflection of the relationship to Social Climate of that part of Type of Program not accounted for by academic ability, namely, status characteristics. Using the latter interpretation, these findings confirmed the notion that high status students in West Germany are more cynical about their schools than students in other countries.

6. In addition to the general finding concerning rote and ritual as negative correlates of Dissent Toleration, student independence appeared as a relatively strong positive predictor in the Federal Republic. It is not clear why this dimension appeared in the Federal Republic while student activism appeared in the United States. It is possible that student independence is simply another avenue to "internal control." As such, it could diminish

---

[1] For further evidence of this assertion, see S.B. Robinsohn and J.C. Kuhlmann, "Two Decades of Non-Reform in West German Education," *Comparative Education Review* 11, No. 3 (1976), pp. 313–317, 324–325 and OECD, *Review of National Policies for Education: Germany*, Paris, 1972.

defensive reactions to dissent just as political activism was thought to do in the United States.

The cross-national differences which appear with respect to these dimensions may also reflect the existence of somewhat different notions of dissent toleration in the two countries, notions which are consistent with their general political cultures (Almond and Verba, 1963). In the United States, the active component of dissent toleration was more evident than in West Germany, i.e., "a good citizen tries to change things in government" was more strongly related to the tolerance scale in the former country than in the latter. On the other hand, in the FRG, dissent toleration appeared to be endorsed more as an abstract concept.

In this light, it is not surprising that social climate dimensions indicating student political initiative are better predictors of Dissent Toleration in the United States than in West Germany. Moreover, it is not surprising that the "independence of thought" dimensions are better predictors of Dissent Toleration in the FRG, where dissent toleration was viewed in more abstract terms.

7. Student initiative and student equality were dimensions which in West Germany were negatively related to Civics Knowledge. The reason for this is unclear. It may be that both were characteristics of low status schools, or it may be that where these dimensions were strong there was sufficient disruption of the learning process to cause lower achievement. It would be interesting to examine these findings in more detail in light of a rather turbulent period of West German educational history, the early 1970's.

8. The contextual analysis for the FRG revealed some important findings. When the average perception of the school climate was substituted for the individual perceptions, the relationship between Social Climate and Civics Knowledge shrank to almost nothing. One interpretation of this phenomenon is that the former correlations were a reflection of the impact of performance characteristics on individual perceptions: that is, individuals who performed well in schools tended to perceive their school in a more favorable light than those who performed poorly.

With School Social Climate eliminated as a predictor of Civics Knowledge in the contextual analysis, the only other significant predictors were Word Knowledge, Type of Program and Conflict with the Family. These findings seem to suggest that in West Germany personal background variables override school quality variables in accounting for learning differences, a conclusion similar to that reached by Weiler (1971). The fact remains, however, that higher achievers do perceive greater emphasis on concepts, less emphasis on ritual, more independence of thought, and so forth in their schools. Such dimensions, if not determinants of civics achievement, are certainly correlates of it. Longitudinal research is needed in order to demonstrate conclusively whether one could increase civics knowledge among youth in the FRG by changing social climate dimensions.

Educational Policy Implications

Educators and legislators in both the United States and the Federal Republic of Germany who are interested in promoting more tolerant attitudes towards political dissent would do well to consider the strong positive relationship between civics knowledge and dissent toleration revealed by this research. There is certainly nothing revolutionary about this finding. To be sure, the concept of an enlightened electorate's being the backbone of democratic politics is one of the fundamental ideals of liberal democracy. Yet it is comforting in these years of growing political cynicism to find empirical confirmation of this ideal in two large Western democracies. This research demonstrates that the more individuals know about democratic institutions and processes, the more tolerant of dissent they are likely to be.

One way to increase dissent toleration, then, is to increase the student's knowledge of civics. Methods for increasing civics knowledge have been suggested by previous investigations as well as by the present research. They include increasing basic verbal skills, increasing the number and changing the content of civic education courses, and changing the social climate in which the courses are taught.

The present study shows clearly that the students with greater verbal ability are those who score highest on the Civics Achievement Test. It is likely that any school input which could increase a student's verbal ability would also positively affect a student's performance on such tests. It is not clear, however, that such improved performance is an index of anything other than better test-taking ability. But even if a student does not learn more about political processes and institutions, his improved performance on tests is likely to enhance his self-esteem and thus influence a variety of social attitudes including, presumably, dissent toleration (Sniderman, 1974). Unfortunately, previous research, including some from IEA sources (Thorndike, 1973) has indicated that basic verbal skills are only marginally influenced by formal schooling. This does not mean that schools should abandon all attempts to increase students' verbal abilities. It only means that such efforts are bound to have very marginal effects on such outcomes as increased tolerance of dissent.

Increasing the number of required civics courses is another possible avenue to increased civics knowledge. A number of studies (Langton and Jennings, 1968; Litt, 1963; Azrael, 1965) have demonstrated, however, that students in both the United States and Europe are easily saturated by such courses. The recent review of adolescent political education by Jennings and Niemi (1974) shows that the number of "social studies" courses a student takes is only weakly related to increases in political learning and tolerance.

To some extent, this is a reflection on the *content* of traditional secondary school civic education courses. Langton and Jennings (1968) indicate that much of what is taught in such courses is redundant with things learned in other places. Dawson and Prewitt (1969) point out that such courses are frequently geared to "political indoctrination" rather than "civic education." By its very nature, indoctrination stresses the value of consensus and order and deemphasizes (or discredits) the value of political dissent and free inquiry. Such courses not only discourage political learning but contribute to increased dogmatism in some students, increased cynicism in others. In order to contribute meaningfully to increased civics knowledge, courses will need to be made more interesting, more balanced, more critical and more relevant to students' lives.

This leads us to the final avenue to increased civics knowledge: the social climate in which civics instruction takes place. It is appropriate once again to quote Patrick's (1967) statement, that "political education programs would have a greater influence upon the formation of 'democratic' attitudes if they were conducted in an atmosphere conducive to inquiry and open-mindedness." The social climate scales in this study were created to provide a direct measure of the extent to which schools provided such an atmosphere. Data from the United States and the Federal Republic of Germany provided evidence that school social climate does relate to civics achievement, independent of personal and social background factors. In both countries, higher scores on the civics knowledge test were related to a concept-oriented academic climate and low levels of patriotic rituals. Also, in the USA, opportunities for student initiative in discussions and decision making, and involvement in democratically run peer groups were independently related to civics knowledge. In the FRG, students' opportunities for argumentation with teachers on politically-oriented topics were related to civics knowledge.

Teachers and administrators in both countries could use these findings in a variety of ways. They could act directly, by emphasizing such aspects as concept learning, independent thinking, and student initiative and deemphasizing harsh teacher control and patriotic rituals. Furthermore, by recognizing that the environments they work in and *help to create* are measurable and changeable, they could periodically assess the social climates of their schools, and use the results to help pinpoint and change aspects which are inconsistent with their ideals and objectives. The perceptions of the students are the best gauge of the social climate features which directly influence student behavior and attitudes. Such perceptions could indicate to teachers and administrators whether or not their instructional programs were "coming across" in the ways they expected.

Schooling leads to all kinds of unintended effects on students—some positive, some negative. An example of a negative effect is the lowered self-esteem experienced by some students as they compare their performance with that of others. Other kinds of unintended consequences relate to school climates. For example, many teachers instruct their students on the virtues of free speech in classroom environments where students are afraid to speak "out of turn" or give their own opinions. The real message in such classrooms is that free expression is dangerous or disruptive or at best, risky. The implication for school policy here is that teachers and administrators pay at least as much attention to the *social context* in which subjects are presented as to the *content* of the subject matter.

An example of a positive unintended effect of education is found in the present research. Achievement in civics in the two countries is directly related to various aspects of the social climate. Dissent toleration in the two countries is directly related to the same aspects. This means that the same features of the environment which encourage more effective learning also influence more tolerant attitudes. An implication of this finding for policy is that educators need not institute special programs to teach tolerance. Increased tolerance appears as a "by-product" of more effective learning. This finding is consistent with that of Holsinger (1972), who found that Brazilian school children developed "modern values" as a result of their exposure to modern social and physical structures in the school environment, not because they were explicitly *taught* to be modern. Furthermore, those classrooms which were the most effective in promoting learning gains were also the most effective "modernizers". Likewise, in the present research, schools which are the most effective in conveying civics knowledge are also the most effective in socializing dissent toleration.

Educators can also use the results of the present study to help combat the growing wave of pessimism concerning the school's capacity to influence worthwhile outcomes. Distinguished scholars such as Ralf Dahrendorf (1967) of West Germany and James Coleman (1966) of the United States shook their countries' educational communities in the mid-sixties by pronouncing that schools had very little influence on learning once family background factors were taken into account. Partly in reaction to such pronouncements, a number of scholars have recently succeeded in defining more clearly and measuring more carefully the dimensions which distinguish one school from another. In particular, school climate research (Walberg and Anderson, 1968; Trickett and Moos, 1973; McDill and Rigsby, 1973; Holsinger, 1972) has demonstrated that there are substantial qualitative differences between schools and that these differences relate to student outcome factors such as achievement, satisfaction, educational aspirations and attitudinal modernity. The present study contributes additional collaborative evidence that school quality factors play a role in the development of student values.

This study can also contribute to a growing awareness of the importance of viewing educational processes in cross-national perspective. In order to understand variations in educational outcomes, it is not enough just to acknowledge that learning takes place within the context of a unique social system, the school. For the school system itself is embedded within an ever-expanding network of social systems. In the broadest sense, examining education *in context* means considering not only school environments, but community and state environments, regional environments, economic and political systems, historical contexts, national settings and the international community. Obviously, it is impossible to consider all of these contexts simultaneously. It is, however, possible to study the interrelationships of some of those systems taken a few at a time. This study has considered the social system of the school as it is embedded within two different national systems. It has followed the logic of Przeworski and Teune (1970) who stress the value of comparing similar national systems which nevertheless vary along theoretically interesting dimensions.

One of the main results of this comparison was the discovery of significant systemic differences in the area of school stratification. Although both national systems group students according to ability and aspirations to some extent, the type of academic program one attends in the Federal Republic of Germany is heavily influenced by family background factors and has an almost overwhelming effect on student attitude development. The cross-national differences along these lines were sufficiently strong that two different models were used to describe attitude development in the two countries: a resource conversion model for the United States and a stratification model for the Federal Republic.

Policy decisions in the two countries would need to take these broad systemic differences into account. For example, in the United States, teaching more students to be tolerant of dissent means influencing the process of resource conversion at some point. For some students, this may mean helping them to convert their native abilities into the kind of knowledge which relates to tolerance; for others, this may mean influencing the pre-school years in such a way that they have sufficient native ability to convert into future opportunities.

In West Germany, however, helping more students to be tolerant may require moving more students into the high status programs (e.g., the *Gymnasium*). Alternatively, it may mean leveling the status differences between school types, either by conferring more importance upon lower status programs or by moving towards a more comprehensive school system. A comprehensive system would not necessarily produce more tolerant students. Such a system would, however, put students from all social strata into a position where individual resources and socialization experiences in the schools assumed far greater importance in the process of attitude and value development.

Concluding Remarks

Throughout the pages of this chapter I have suggested a number of topics for future research. I have suggested that questions concerning school climate *impacts* need to be analyzed using longitudinal and/or field experimental designs so that doubts about causal ordering and selection effects can be resolved. I have also suggested the need for more in-depth studies of the historical contexts in which schools and students were interacting in the early 1970's.

In addition to the above, another direction for future research would be to consider the interaction between individuals and the social environment in producing differing levels of dissent toleration. The present study proceeded as if the social climate influenced all students in the same manner, regardless of personality differences. Although this may be true on the average, it obscures a number of very interesting variations. For example, some students, because of low self-esteem or shyness, may react with high levels of anxiety to classroom environments which emphasize independent thought and confrontation with controversial issues. Such anxiety could actually cause a decrease in one's respect for the value of dissent. In sum, there is no single optimum classroom environment for all people. In future research, personality as well as social climate variables need to be brought together in a more interactive model.

Yet another direction for future research would involve returning to the original theoretical model of the study. In doing so, one could examine simultaneously the intervening effects of the personality structure (dogmatism) and the idea system (political cognitions). Both variables have been shown to be related to dissent toleration. But how do they interact? Can non-dogmatic people who know very little about democratic institutions and processes still score high on a test of dissent toleration? How would highly informed dogmatic people score? Are the variables additive? That is, are those who are both highly informed and non-dogmatic the most tolerant of all? Such questions can only be addressed when both kinds of variables are available for analysis in the same study.

Finally, it would be interesting to replicate a study such as this in other national settings. In less developed countries, for example, schools are assumed to have more dramatic effects on value change. Would the climate of the schools in such countries have a greater impact on values such as dissent toleration even though the political institutions are less prepared to cope with social conflict? Is increased tolerance for dissent one of the destabilizing consequences of schooling in traditional countries, or can the schools, by maintaining highly controlling environments, promote intolerance and acceptance of repressive practices? If increased tolerance is an inevitable result of public schooling (just as "modernity" appears to be) should not government officials in developing countries be more concerned about developing institutions for channelling political conflict than they often appear to be?

Such questions are important in a world which in the 1970's appears to be turning to more authoritarian solutions to its political dilemmas. Institutional weaknesses are certainly responsible for some of the difficulties governments have in channeling political conflict, particularly in the less developed countries. Yet individual intolerance is also responsible.

Democratic nations have placed much of the burden for eradicating political intolerance upon their public school systems. The educational community's success in meeting this challenge depends upon how well they teach democratic principles and this depends, at least in part, upon the kinds of learning environments they create.

Appendix

A. Table A.1. Participation in Civic Education Survey by Country and Population.
B. Civics Knowledge Questionnaire
C. Dissent Toleration Items
D. School Social Climate Items
E. Background Questions

A. TABLE A.1. Participation in Civic Education Survey by Country and Population

	Population		
	I	II	IV
Country	(10-year-olds)	(14-year-olds)	(Final year of Secondary school)
Federal Republic of Germany	x	x	x
Finland		x	x
Ireland		x	x
Israel	x	x	
Italy	x	x	
Netherlands	x	x	x
New Zealand		x	x
Sweden			x
United States		x	x

B. CIVIC EDUCATION COGNITIVE TEST

Directions:

Each of the questions or incomplete statements in this test is followed by five possible answers. You are to decide which one of these answers is *best*.

Mark your answer by blackening in the appropriate space on the answer card. If you want to change an answer, be sure to erase the old mark completely. You will have 35 minutes to answer the 47 questions in this test. This is *NOT* a test on which you will be graded. Therefore, do *NOT* guess at any answer unless you are fairly sure that you know the answer. If you are unsure of the answer simply leave it blank. Here is the first example:

P1. Which one of the following is a nation?

    A. Tokyo
    B. Australia
    C. Copenhagen
    D. Montreal
    E. Cairo

Since Australia is a nation and the others are only cities, you should choose the answer numbered B. On your answer card you see space B blackened in for you. Now you blacken in the appropriate space on your answer card for the next example:

P2. Which of the following are the capital cities of their countries?

    I. Vienna, Austria
    II. Copenhagen, Denmark
    III. Barcelona, Spain
    IV. Ankara, Turkey
    V. Athens, Greece

    A. I and II only
    B. II and IV only
    C. II, III, and V only
    D. I, II, III, IV and V

The answer to this question in D, because each of these cities, I, II, IV and V, is a capital city. Madrid is the capital of Spain, *NOT* Barcelona. Therefore, number III *CANNOT* be part of the right answer.

Mark only one answer for each question. If you change your mind about an answer, be sure to erase the first mark completely. Do *NOT* spend too much time on any one question. If a question seems too difficult, go on to the next one.

1. Patriotism means that one has affection for his:
    A. friends.
    B. government.
    C. town.
    D. nation.
    E. family.

2. A tax is money that people:
    A. pay as fines in order to provide money for the upkeep of the courts.
    B. give to the poor in order to supply them with food.
    C. put into the bank in order to make banknotes available for the public.
    D. receive from the government in order to meet the costs of living.

E. pay for necessary public services which they enjoy.

3. Which of the following are usually elected by popular vote in your nation?
    A. diplomats.
    B. civil servants.
    C. high court judges.
    D. members of Congress (Parliament, Riksdag, etc.).
    E. public (state) school teachers.

4. Legislative proposals made by congressmen (MP's, etc.) are called:
    A. bills (propositions in Sweden).
    B. resolutions.
    C. comments.
    D. ordinances.
    E. laws.

5. Who can change the speed limits on your public roads?
    A. automobile clubs.
    B. insurance companies.
    C. government officials.
    D. motor car (automobile) manufacturers.
    E. judges.

6. The main purpose of a court is to:
    A. suggest new laws.
    B. supervise criminals after they have served their sentences.
    C. determine how long young people shall stay at school.
    D. regulate speed limits.
    E. try individuals accused of breaking the law.

7. Why is it important to have more than one person involved in decision-making and passing the laws (bills, propositions, etc.) in any nation?
    A. It provides government posts for more people.
    B. It is following established practice.
    C. It prevents some mistakes and provides for public discussion of other points of view.
    D. It looks better in the press to decide things in this way.
    E. It enables more people to become better acquainted with the law.

8. In order to achieve its aims and program, the primary purpose of a political party is to:
    A. win elections and exert political power.
    B. raise money for the government.
    C. lower taxes for the poor.
    D. prevent public debate of controversial issues.
    E. ensure regular elections.

9. Suppose you are a voter. In order to choose the party or the candidate for whom you wish to vote, which of the following procedures would help you to obtain the most useful information?
    A. telephone or write to each candidate and ask their opinions.
    B. ask your friends how they are voting and vote the same way.
    C. study the qualifications, ideas, and records of the candidates and parties.
    D. read the literature of just one candidate or party but not the others.

E. look at the photographs of each party's candidates in the newspapers.

10. "I don't think politics or election results affect my own life very much." This statement is more likely to be made by someone who:
    A. is a regular contributor to a political party of his choice.
    B. rarely follows political campaigns and congressional (parliamentary) proceedings.
    C. follows political campaigns very closely.
    D. encourages other citizens to participate in politics.
    E. attends work irregularly.

11. Which of the following activities has the United Nations Organization undertaken?
    I. the imposition of custom duties.
    II. the giving of assistance to underdeveloped nations.
    III. the issuing of passports to tourists.
    IV. the keeping of the peace in trouble spots.
    V. the imposition of taxes on individuals in your nation.

    A. I and II only
    B. I and V only
    C. II and IV only
    D. III and V only
    E. IV and V only

12. Which of the following is a part of the United Nations Organization?
    A. The World Health Organization.
    B. The Organization of African States.
    C. The Arab League.
    D. The Olympic Games International Committee.
    E. The Boy Scouts and Girl Scouts (Guides).

13. You would find the MOST accurate description of the organization, structure, and functions of the United Nations in the:
    A. Universal Declaration of Human Rights.
    B. Statutes of the International Court of Justice.
    C. UNESCO Charter.
    D. Bretton Woods Agreement.
    E. United Nations Charter.

Question 14. refers to the following drawing:

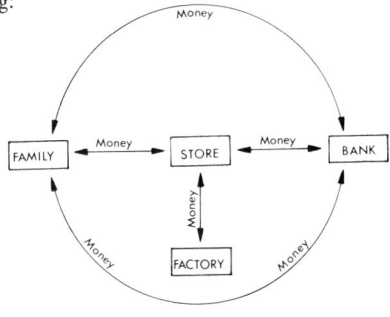

«The Family, the Factory, the Bank, and Money»

14. Which is the best description of the preceding drawing?
    A. how banks are important to society.
    B. how workers get their money.
    C. how money circulates.
    D. how factories get their money from shops.
    E. how factories depend on loans from banks.

15. In which of the following nations is the population most rapidly outgrowing the supplies of food, clothing, and shelter?
    A. Japan.
    B. Mexico.
    C. Cananda.
    D. India.
    E. Zambia.

16. Suppose that it is agreed that building and maintaining a road (highway) system is the responsibility of your government (local, state, national, etc.). Which of the following is LEAST related to fulfiling that responsibility?
    A. erecting traffic signs and signals and keeping the road clear of obstacles.
    B. levying taxes to maintain the roads (highways).
    C. closing roads (highways) during emergencies.
    D. punishing those who violate traffic regulations.
    E. manufacturing vehicles and automobile accessories.

17. In most nations nearly all adult men and women are required to:
    A. pay taxes.
    B. speak the same language.
    C. marry and have a family.
    D. pay dues to a political party.
    E. serve in the armed forces.

18. A group of people sharing a territory, sharing some political interests, and ruled over by a government is a:
    A. family.
    B. political party.
    C. trade union.
    D. political league (union).
    E. state.

19. In a democratic political system, which of the following ought to govern the nation?
    A. one strong leader.
    B. a small group of well-educated people.
    C. popularly elected representatives.
    D. large land owners and important businessmen.
    E. experts on government and political affairs.

20. Which of the following sentences shows ONE important feature of a democratic way of thinking or acting?
    A. Children should obey their parents without discussion or hesitation.
    B. Only a few persons should take part in public affairs and politics.
    C. Certain public decisions should be voted on after free and informed discussion and debate.

D. The leaders of the state, not the citizens, should decide what is best for the citizenry.
E. The job of a factory worker is to do what he is told without question.

21. Which of the following is an important activity carried on by both your national and local governments?
    A. issuing postage stamps.
    B. issuing passports.
    C. issuing currency.
    D. building roads.
    E. sending ambassadors to foreign countries.

22. The government of your nation is NOT responsible for:
    A. printing postage stamps.
    B. minting coins.
    C. publishing newspapers sold every day.
    D. granting passports.
    E. issuing pilots' licenses.

23. Mr. A. refuses to pay Mr. B. $2,000 (£1,000, etc.) for goods supplied a year ago. What should Mr. B. do to obtain his money?
    A. hire a lawyer and sue Mr. A. for the money in court.
    B. ask a judge to send Mr. A. to prison as a debtor.
    C. have Mr. A. declared as bankrupt.
    D. report the matter to the police as a crime.
    E. threaten Mr. A. with personal harm.

24. General elections are held in democratic nations mainly to:
    A. educate the public in political affairs.
    B. ensure that people will vote.
    C. make certain that the governing party will change frequently.
    D. allow the people to review and re-express their political preferences.
    E. keep taxes at a lower level.

25. Which of the following nations have largely socialized economies and governmental systems in which political debate and competition are carried on inside the single national political party?
    A. Canada and Switzerland.
    B. Austria and Australia.
    C. Japan and Israel.
    D. Norway and Greece.
    E. The Soviet Union and Yugoslavia.

26. Which of these units of the United Nations Organization has as its chief goal the keeping of peace between nations?
    A. Food and Agricultural Organization.
    B. Security Council.
    C. International Labor Organisation.
    D. Economic and Social Council.
    E. Trusteeship Council.

27. What was achieved by the former League of Nations?
    A. close cooperation between the Soviet Union and the United States.
    B. the prevention of many international aggressive acts.

     C.   the securing of universal disarmament on a trial basis.
     D.   international cooperation in trying to solve certain economic and social problems.
     E.   the creation of an international state.

28. In the United Nations Character the peoples who founded the United Nations Organization promised to:

     A.   prevent the use of armed force except in the common interest of member states.
     B.   grant independence and self-government to African nations.
     C.   do away with tariffs and other barriers to trade.
     D.   restore national boundaries as they were before 1939.
     E.   stabilize the world economy.

29. Which of the following is a member of the European Common Market?

     A.   Belgium.
     B.   Switzerland.
     C.   Greece.
     D.   Austria.
     E.   Spain.

30. Which of the following ideas is NOT in the United Nations Declaration of Human Rights?

     A.   Everyone has the right to freedom and personal security.
     B.   No one may be forced to join an organization.
     C.   No one may be arrested, imprisoned or forced to leave his country without reason.
     D.   Everyone has the right, if his family is in danger, to disobey national laws.
     E.   Everyone has the right to equal pay for the same work.

31. A customs duty is a tax on:

     A.   a gift of money sent from abroad.
     B.   goods brought into a nation.
     C.   aliens who live in a nation.
     D.   property owned in another region.
     E.   corporate profits of foreign owned businesses.

32. A major purpose of a labor (trade) union is to:

     A.   establish a tax system for workers.
     B.   bring production to the highest possible level.
     C.   further the rights and interests of workers.
     D.   defend the rights and interests of employers.
     E.   encourage workers to learn about people of other nations.

33. Which of these services is NOT correctly matched with the level of government (local or national) which usually finances it in your nation?

     A.   military defense – national.
     B.   postal service – national.
     C.   garbage collection – local.
     D.   social security program – national.
     E.   street lighting – national.

34. A protective tariff on imports is designed primarily by a nation to help:

     A.   foreign consumers in the nation.

B. government employees in the nation.
C. producers and manufactures in the nation.
D. small taxpayers and landowners in the nation.
E. defense industries in the nation.

35. A school class is clearly able to decide which of the following on its own by voting?

    A. the reason for a classmate's illness and absence from school.
    B. the need for more homework during the school year.
    C. the price that shall be charged for school books.
    D. the salary which shall be paid to the teacher.
    E. the person who shall act as the class representative or officer.

36. Which of the following is the best way to judge the accuracy of sources of information about public problems?

    A. believe widely expressed points of view which can be easily understood.
    B. check the information against other available sources.
    C. rely upon the opinions of important people.
    D. be automatically negative to new ideas and new sources of information.
    E. verify if the sources are in accord with established national traditions.

37. Which of the following statements about solving social problems is most accurate?

    A. Every nation has completely different problems.
    B. Most problems will be solved whether or not one does anything about them.
    C. Since social change is always taking place, new problems constantly arise and require new solutions.
    D. Mankind's basic problem has been how to rise above material well-being.
    E. Mankind has succeeded in solving almost all of its basic economic, social and political problems.

38. Which of the following statements about individual freedom in a democracy is most accurate?

    A. The free man can do anything he wants.
    B. Liberty consists in asserting oneself without taking others into account.
    C. There is no limit to the liberty of the citizens in a democratic society.
    D. A person's freedom ends at the point where society says it may start hurting other people.
    E. The poor and the illiterate have individual freedom but no responsibility.

39. Parliamentary government means that:

    A. the leaders of the government are selected from the leading party or parties in parliament.
    B. the system of government is based upon limited or restricted right to vote.
    C. most important parliamentary decisions are prepared following consultation among all the parties.
    D. parliament is divided into two chambers.
    E. no more than two parties are represented in parliament.

40. Other things being equal, higher prices for goods in short supply are more likely to result if people:

    A. save more of their money.
    B. try to buy the goods which are in short supply.
    C. import cheaper goods in general.
    D. export more goods in general.

E. produce more of the goods which are in short supply.
41. Your national government obtains the largest portion of its revenue from which of the following tax sources?
   A. personal income taxes.
   B. corporation taxes.
   C. sales taxes.
   D. tobacco and liquor (excise) taxes.
   E. customs duties (tariffs).
42. Which of the following most fully defines the meaning of the word citizen?
   A. He actively works in politics.
   B. He obeys the laws of the nation in which he lives.
   C. He pays taxes in the nation in which he lives.
   D. He has certain rights and responsibilities in his nation.
   E. He is literate.
43. If there were a high protective tariff in Japan upon Swiss watches, who would most directly benefit?
   A. Swiss watchmakers.
   B. Japanese citizens who buy Swiss watches.
   C. Japanese customs officials.
   D. Japanese watchmakers.
   E. The Swiss government.
44. Today national laws prohibit children from working in certain jobs before a certain age. Of the following, which is a major argument for these laws?
   A. to make adults earn enough to support their families.
   B. to give children an opportunity to learn and protect them from harm.
   C. to avoid the production of inferior goods.
   D. to follow the children's desire to stay in school rather than going to work.
   E. to free the children from difficulties of learning the necessary techniques of labor.
45. Which of the following constitutes the clearest *violation* of civil liberties in a democratic political system?
   A. An armed policeman in uniform enters a place of worship during a service.
   B. A policeman breaks up a private meeting where people are criticizing government policies.
   C. A policeman arrests members of a group who have plotted an armed uprising against the government.
   D. A government official sues a columnist who criticized him in a newspaper article.
   E. A person carrying an unregistered revolver is arrested and fined.
46. In relation to the achievements of the United Nations to date, it would be most correct to say that:
   A. nothing of lasting importance has been achieved.
   B. there has been more progress in settling major political disputes than in promoting economic and social co-operation.
   C. most progress has been made in bringing about universal disarmament.
   D. there has been more progress in the work of the specialized agencies than in settling major political disputes.
   E. all of its major goals were achieved long ago.

47. Why is it that in many Western democratic political systems, interest and pressure groups rarely evolve into major political parties?
   A. They prefer to work in private.
   B. They could not win an election without broadening their structure and function.
   C. Their leaders realize that it is against the national interest for such groups to control the government.
   D. Their leaders fear that members who gain political office will work against the interests of the group.
   E. They are prevented from doing so by strict regulatory legislation.

C. DISSENT TOLERATION ITEMS

These questions were taken from a larger set of items in the Civic Education Affective Questionnaire. Only questions used in the current study are listed here. The full questionnaire is given in Oppenheim and Torney (1974). The numbers above each question are the IEA Data Bank Merge File numbers.

Questions:

Here are some things that have been said about the way our nation should be governed. You may agree with some of them and disagree with others; sometimes you will agree or disagree *strongly;* at other times you will feel uncertain or have no opinion. Please look at each statement, and then put a tick (✓) in one of the columns beside it to show how you feel about it.

	Strongly Agree	Agree	I have no opinion	Disagree	Strongly Disagree
Q7CA025. Newspapers and magazines should be allowed to print anything they want except military secrets					
Q7CA029. People should be allowed to come together whenever they like					
Q7CA031. Citizens must always be free to criticize the government					
Q7CA033. People who disagree with the government should be allowed to meet and hold public protests					
Q7CA042. When something is wrong, it is better to complain to the authorities about it than to keep quiet					
Q7CA043. It is good for a government to be frequently criticized					
Q7CA047. The people in power know best					

Q7CA051.

It is wrong to criticize our government .....

Q7CA054.

People should not criticize the government; it only interrupts the government's work ...

There are lots of different people in our nation. Do you think they should all have the same rights and freedoms as everyone else or should they be treated differently? Please put a tick (✓) for every group to show how *you* think they should be treated.

They should have:	More rights and freedoms than everyone else	Exactly the same as everyone else	Fewer rights and freedoms than everyone else	I don't know
Q7CA068. Colored people (substitute national phrasing)				
Q7CA070. Communists				
Q7CA075. People with anti- (insert name of mother nation) views				

Imagine that you had to explain what a good citizen is, or what a good citizen ought to do. Please read each sentence, then put a tick (✓) under the heading 'Good Citizen' if that is what *you* mean by a good citizen. If the sentence does NOT help to explain what you mean by a good citizen, put a tick under 'No'. If you are not sure, put a tick under 'Not sure'.

A good citizen:	Good Citizen	Not Sure	No
Q7CA097. Tries to change things in the government			

D. SCHOOL SOCIAL CLIMATE ITEMS

Listed below are the items, by social climate dimension, included in any version of the School Social Climate scales.

1. Classroom Equality

    Here are some statements about things that happen in some schools. How often does each of these happen in *your* school?

          A. Always
          B. Often
          C. Sometimes
          D. Rarely
          E. Never

    There are five columns from which to choose your answer. Please read each statement then put a tick (✓) in the column that shows how often each of these things really happens in *your* school.

	Always	Often	Sometimes	Rarely	Never
Q7CB58. Every member of our class has the same privileges..	___	___	___	___	___
Q7CB63. The better students get special favors from teachers............	___	___	___	___	___
Q7CB68. Certain students are favored by the teachers more than the rest.........	___	___	___	___	___

2. Peer Group Interaction

    Q7CB35.

    Suppose that you and your friends are playing a game, and some of you want to change one of the rules of the game or make a new rule. How would the group decide? (Tick the *one* that happens most often.)

    A. _____ We would talk about it until we all agreed.

    B. _____ There are generally one or two persons in the group who would decide.

    C. _____ We would go and ask someone to decide the rules for us.

    D. _____ We would try the new rule and see if it makes for a better game.

    E. _____ We would talk about it, and then take a vote.

Q7CB36.

Suppose that you and your friends were planning to go on a hike or a trip in your spare time. How would the group decide where to go? (Tick the *one* that happens most often.)

A. _____ We would talk about it until we all agreed.

B. _____ There are generally one or two persons in the group who would decide.

C. _____ We would go and ask someone to decide for us.

D. _____ We would accept the advice of someone who had been there before.

E. _____ We would talk about it, and then take a vote.

Q7CB37.

Suppose you and your friends had a club, and the club needed a leader. How would your group choose the leader? (Tick the *one* that happens most often.)

A. _____ We would talk about it until we all agreed.

B. _____ A good leader would come forward naturally.

C. _____ We would talk about it, and then take a vote.

D. _____ We would try out different leaders until we found the best one.

E. _____ We would ask someone to decide for us.

Q7CB38.

Suppose that you and your friends had collected some money. How would your group decide what to use the money for? (Tick the *one* that happens most often.)

A. _____ We would talk about it until we all agreed.

B. _____ The leaders of our group would decide what to do.

C. _____ We would go and ask someone to decide for us.

D. _____ We would talk about it, and then take a vote.

E. _____ We would wait until we knew more and had some new ideas.

3. Independence of Thought

Here are some statements about things that happen in some schools. How often does each of these happen in your school?

	Always	Often	Sometimes	Rarely	Never
Q7CB60. Teachers try to get students to speak freely and openly in class	_____	_____	_____	_____	_____

Q7CB61.

Students can feel free to disagree openly with their teachers..............

Q7CB65.

Students are encouraged to make up their own minds...

Q7CB70.

Our teachers respect our opinions and encourage us to express them......

4. Academic Climate

	Always	Often	Sometimes	Rarely	Never

Q7CB74.

Causes and explanations of social or historical events are more important than remembering names or dates..........

Q7CB76.

In history or civics classes we must learn dates or definitions by heart..

5. Political Environment

	Always	Often	Sometimes	Rarely	Never

Q7CB78.

Students bring up current political events for discussion in class....

6. Ritual Climate of Classrooms

	Always	Often	Sometimes	Rarely	Never
Q7CB56. We sing songs about our country in class..........					
Q7CB59. We sing our national anthem in school...					
Q7CB64. We participate in a ceremony with our national flag in school (e.g. say the Pledge of Allegiance)...					
Q7CB69. There are pictures of national leaders in our classrooms.........					

7. Teacher Control

    The items below are statements about the things you do and the things that happen in your school. Decide whether each one is *generally* true for you or for your school. If you agree with it, choose A; if you disagree, choose B.

    Q63A02.

    Students in this school rarely express opinions which differ from the teacher's.

    A. Agree
    B. Disagree

    Q63A05.

    The teachers often make you feel small.

    A. Agree
    B. Disagree

8. Student Power

    a. From Teacher Questionnaire:
       Items 30–37 list some activities which schools could provide for their students. In each case indicate whether you think such activities should or should not be provided.

	A Should be Provided	B Should not be Provided
TNC31. Take part in making decisions about discipline	A	B

b. From School Questionnaire:

SN3107.

To what extent do each of the following groups participate in making school policies and rules?

STUDENTS: Not at all_____   To some extent _____ To a great extent _____

E. BACKGROUND QUESTIONS

1. Parental Socioeconomic Status

    FOCC.

    Please write your father's occupation. _____

    (If your father is dead, give your gaurdian's occupation, or, if you do not have a gaurdian, give your father's occupation before he died.)

    On the lines below, describe his occupation as clearly as you can. Please state the duties he performs and for whom he works. For example, if he is a "salesman," tell what he sells and where he works.

    MED.

    How many years of full-time education (including school, college, university, etc.) did your mother receive? (*indicate one*)

    A. 0 years   B. $>0 \leqslant 5$ C. $>5 \leqslant 10$

    D. $>10 \leqslant 15$ E. >15

    FED.

    How many years of full-time education (including school, college, university, etc.) did your father receive? (*indicate one*)

    A. 0 years   B. $>0 \leqslant 5$ C. $>5 \leqslant 10$

    D. $>10 \leqslant 15$ E. >15

2. Verbal Ability

    The following is the WORD KNOWLEDGE TEST, used at the 14-year-old level:

    WORD KNOWLEDGE TEST

    Directions

    In this test words are given to you in pairs. In each pair, the two words have something in common. You must decide whether the words mean nearly the *same* thing or nearly the *opposite* thing with respect to what they have in common.

    If you think the words have the *same* meaning, blacken in the oval marked " + " on your answer card.

    If you think the words have the *opposite* meaning, blacken in the oval marked "0" on your answer card.

    Here is an example:

            high   low   ⊕   ⓪

    The two words "high" and "low" both refer to height. However, they are nearly *opposite* in meaning. Therefore you should blacken in the oval marked "0" on your answer card like this:

        ⊕   ⓪

    For each of the following pairs, blacken in either "+" or "0". You should attempt every item for which you think you know the answer, but do not guess if you have no idea of the answer.

Word Knowledge Test

1.	savory	insipid	+	0
2.	informed	unaware	+	0
3.	precarious	stable	+	0
4.	rapid	sluggish	+	0
5.	supple	malleable	+	0
6.	associate	partner	+	0
7.	decoration	ornamentation	+	0
8.	mute	voluble	+	0
9.	prosperity	opulence	+	0
10.	ordered	confused	+	0
11.	prohibited	forbidden	+	0
12.	boastfulness	modesty	+	0
13.	wealthy	impoverished	+	0
14.	adjacent	contiguous	+	0
15.	create	originate	+	0
16.	garrulous	taciturn	+	0
17.	expatiate	harangue	+	0
18.	rare	habitual	+	0
19.	benevolent	intolerant	+	0
20.	vague	precise	+	0
21.	wise	judicious	+	0
22.	acquire	dispel	+	0
23.	ancient	antique	+	0
24.	abstruse	explicit	+	0
25.	loosen	relax	+	0
26.	despise	scorn	+	0
27.	flagrant	obvious	+	0
28.	gauge	measure	+	0
29.	paltry	exorbitant	+	0
30.	absolute	relative	+	0
31.	everlasting	permanent	+	0
32.	conformity	dissimilarity	+	0
33.	converge	approach	+	0
34.	consecrate	dedicate	+	0
35.	deny	repeal	+	0
36.	variable	inconstant	+	0
37.	bounty	generosity	+	0
38.	delicate	tactful	+	0
39.	repudiate	disavow	+	0
40.	obvious	indisputable	+	0

3. Type of Educational Program
   a. USA
      What type of program are you currently enrolled in? (Check one)
      A. _____ General
      B. _____ Vocational or commercial
      C. _____ Academic
      D. _____ Other
   b. FRG
      What type of school are you currently enrolled in? (Check one)
      A. _____ Hauptschule (Volksschule)
      B. _____ Realschule
      C. _____ Gymnasium
      D. _____ Other

4. Religious Activity
   Here is a list of things which young people sometimes do, or think of doing. Read each one, and then put a tick in the column which is right for *you*. Remember that your answers are CONDIFIDENTIAL, so be as truthful as you can — but don't boast.

	I have never though about this	I have thought about doing this but I have NOT done it.	and I have actually done it.
Q7CB44. Joining the church choir or some other church activity............			

5. Conflict with the Family
   On the whole, do your political opinions agree with those of your parents, teachers or friends, or do you have different political ideas? Put *one* tick on each line.

	I don't know what his or her political ideas are	I agree a lot with	I agree a little with	I mostly disagree with	I am not sure of my own opinions
Q7CB24. My father....					
Q7CB25. My mother...					

131

Here is a list of things which young people sometimes do, or think of doing. Read each one, and then put a tick in the column which is right for *you*. Remember that your answers are CONFIDENTIAL, so be as truthful as you can —— but don't boast.

	I have never thought about this	I have thought about doing this	
		but I have NOT done it.	and I have actually done it.

Q7CB41.

Being rude to your parents . . . .

Q7CB43.

Leaving the house in the evening without permission . . . .

Q7CB45.

Hurting your parents' feelings . . . .

Q7CB47.

Deliberately doing things which older people don't approve of . . . .

Q7CB54.

Being independent of your family . . .

Educational Expectations

EDEXP.

After this year, how many more years of full-time education do you *expect* to receive? (*indicate one*)

A.   0 years   B. $\leqslant 2$ C. $>2 \leqslant 5$

D. $>5 \leqslant 8$ E. >8

Bibliography

Adorno, T.W.; Else Frenkel-Brunswik; Daniel J. Levinson and R. Nevitt Sanford. *The Authoritarian Personality.* New York: Harper and Bros., 1950.

Almond, Gabriel A. and Sidney Verba. *The Civic Culture: Political Attitudes and Democracy in Five Nations.* Princeton: Princeton University Press, 1963.

Anderson, Gary J. "Effects of Classroom Social Climate on Individual Learning." *American Education Research Journal* 7 (1970): 135–152.

Anderson, Gary J. and Herbert J. Walberg. "Learning Environments." In H.J. Walberg (ed.), *Evaluating Educational Performance.* Berkeley: McCutchan, 1974.

Anderson, Richard C. "Learning in Discussions: A Resume of the Authoritarian-Democratic Studies." In Charters and Gage (eds.), *Readings in the Social Psychology of Education.* Boston: Allyn and Bacon, Inc., 1963.

Andrews, J.H.M. "School Organizational Climate: Some Validity Studies." *Canadian Education and Research Digest* 5, no. 4 (1965): 317–334.

Azrael, Jeremy R. "The Soviet Union." In James S. Coleman (ed.), *Education and Political Development.* Princeton: Princeton University Press, 1965.

Bachman, Jerald G., et al. *Youth In Transition, Volume 1.* Ann Arbor, Michigan: Institute for Social Research, The University of Michigan, 1967.

Biddle, B.J. and J.B. Ellena. *Contemporary Research on Teacher Effectiveness.* New York: Holt, Rinehart and Winston, 1964.

Blalock, Herbert M. *Causal Inference in Nonexperimental Research.* Chapel Hill: University of North Carolina Press, 1964.

– "Multiple Indicators and the Causal Approach to Measurement Error." *American Journal of Sociology* 75 (1969): 264–272.

– *Causal Models in the Social Sciences.* Chicago: Aldine Press, 1971.

Bloom, Benjamin S. (ed.) *Taxonomy of Educational Objectives: The Classification of Educational Goals. Handbook 1: Cognitive Domain.* New York: David McKay, 1956.

Blumenthal, Monica D.; Robert L. Kahn and Frank M. Andrews. *Justifying Violence: Attitudes of American Men.* Ann Arbor: Institute for Social Research, University of Michigan, 1972.

Boudon, R. "A New Look at Correlation Analysis." In H.M. Blalock and A.B. Blalock (eds.), *Methodology in Social Research.* New York: McGraw Hill, 1968.

Choppin, Bruce H. *The Correction for Guessing on Objective Tests.* IEA Monograph Studies No. 4. Stockholm: IEA International, 1974.

Christensen, C.M. "Relationships between Pupil Achievement, Affect-Need, Teacher Warmth, and Teacher Permissiveness." *Journal of Educational Psychology* 51 (1960): 169–174.

Christie, Richard and Marie Jahoda. *Studies in the Scope and Method of "The Authoritarian Personality."* Glencoe, Ill.: The Free Press, 1964.

Cogan, M.L. "The Behavior of Teachers and the Productive Behavior of Their Pupils: I." *Journal of Experimental Education* 27 (1958): 89–124.

Coleman, James S. *The Adolescent Society.* New York: Free Press of Glencoe, 1961.

— *Resources for Social Change.* New York: Wiley-Interscience, 1971.
—, et al. *Equality of Educational Opportunity.* Washington: National Center for Educational Statistics, 1966.
Connell, R.W. and Murray Goot. "Science and Ideology in American 'Political Socialization' Research." *Berkeley Journal of Sociology (1972—1973):* 165—193.
Converse, Philip E. "The Nature of Belief Systems in Mass Politics." In David E. Apter (ed.), *Ideology and Discontent.* New York: The Free Press, 1964.
Coser, Lewis. *The Functions of Social Conflict.* New York: The Free Press, 1964.
Dahrendorf, Ralf. *Class and Class Conflict in Industrial Society.* Stanford: Stanford University Press, 1959.
— *Society and Democracy in Germany.* Garden City, New York: Doubleday, 1967.
Dawson, Richard E. and Kenneth Prewitt. *Political Socialization.* Boston: Little, Brown and Co., 1969.
Deutsch, Karl W. "Social Mobilization and Political Development." *American Political Science Review* 55 (1961): 493—514.
Dreeben, Robert. *On What is Learned in School.* Reading, Mass.: Addison-Wesley Publishing Co., 1968.
Duncan, O.D. "Path Analysis: Sociological Examples." *American Journal of Sociology* 72 (1966): 1—16.
— "Contingencies in Constructing Causal Models." In E.F. Borgatta and G.W. Bohrnstedt (eds.), *Sociological Methodology 1969.* San Francisco: Jossey-Bass, 1969, pp. 74—112.
Easton, David. *A Systems Analysis of Political Life.* New York: John Wiley, 1965.
Ehman, Lee H. "An Analysis of the Relationships of Selected Educational Variables with the Political Socialization of High School Students." *American Educational Research Journal* 6 (1969): 559—580.
Fägerlind, Ingemar. *Formal Education and Adult Earnings: A Longitudinal Study on the Economic Benefits of Education.* Stockholm: Almqvist & Wiksell International, 1975.
Federal Republic of Germany Civic Education Committee. *Report.* IEA International, 1967.
Flanders, Ned A. *Analyzing Teacher Behavior.* Reading, Mass.: Addison-Wesley, Co., 1970.
Fox, Thomas Earl. *The Treatment of Social Conflict in Social Studies Textbooks for Grades Three, Five and Nine.* Unpublished Ph.D. Dissertation, Stanford University, 1972.
Furth, Hans G. *Piaget for Teachers.* Edgewood Cliffs, N.J.: Prentice-Hall, Inc., 1970.
Gallagher, James J. "A 'Topic Classification System' for Classroom Interaction." In J.J. Gallagher, et al. (eds.), *Classroom Observation.* Chicago: Rand McNally and Co., 1970.
Gentry, H.W. and J.B. Kenney. "A Comparison of the Organizational Climates of Negro and White Elementary Schools." *The Journal of Psychology* 60 (1965): 171—179.
Gillespie, Judith, A. and Lee H. Ehman. "The School as a Political System." Paper presented at the annual meeting of American Educational Research Association in Chicago, Ill., April 15—19, 1974.
Gordon, R.A. "Issues in Multiple Regression." *American Journal of Sociology* 73

(1968): 592–616.
Grossman, David L. "Educational Climate and Attitudes Toward Dissent: A Study of Political Socialization of Conflict Norms in Adolescents." Unpublished Ph.D. Dissertation, Stanford University, 1976.
Guilford, Joy P. "The Structure of Intellect." *Psychological Bulletin* 53 (1956): 267–293.
Guilford, Joy P. and Benjamin Fruchter. *Fundamental Statistics in Psychology and Education*, 5th Edition. New York: McGraw-Hill, 1973.
Gurr, Ted R. *Why Men Rebel*. Princeton, N.J.: Princeton University Press, 1970.
Halpin, A.W. and D.B. Croft. "The Organizational Climate of Schools." *Administrator's Notebook* 11, no. 7 (1963).
Hess, Robert D. and Judith V. Torney. *The Development of Political Attitudes in Children*. Chicago: Aldine, 1967.
Holmes, Oliver W. *Abrams v. United States*, Supreme Court 17, 20 (1919).
Holsinger, Donald B. *The Elementary School as an Early Socializer of Modern Values*. Unpublished Ph.D. Dissertation, Stanford University, 1972.
Huntington, Samuel P. *Political Order in Changing Societies*. New Haven: Yale University Press, 1968.
Inkeles, Alex. *What is Sociology?* Englewood Cliffs, N.J.: Prentice-Hall, 1964.
Inkeles, Alex and D.J. Levinson, "The Personal System and the Socio-cultural System in Large-scale Organizations." *Sociometry*, 26, no. 2 (1963).
Inkeles, Alex and David Smith. *Becoming Modern: Individual Change in Six Developing Countries*. Cambridge, Mass.: Harvard University Press, 1974.
Jennings, M. Kent; Kenneth P. Langton and Richard G. Niemi. "Effects of the High School Civics Curriculum." In Jennings and Niemi, *The Political Character of Adolescence*. Princeton, N.J.: Princeton University Press, 1974.
Jennings, M. Kent and Richard G. Niemi. *The Political Character of Adolescence: The Influence of Families and Schools*. Princeton, N.J.: Princeton University Press, 1974.
Kerlinger, Fred N. and Elazar J. Pedhazur. *Multiple Regression in Behavioral Research*. New York: Holt, Rinehart and Winston, 1973.
Kob, J. *Erziehung in Elternhaus und Schule*. Stuttgart, 1963.
Lane, Robert E. *Political Ideology: Why the American Common Man Believes What He Does*. Glencoe, Ill.: The Free Press, 1962.
Langton, Kenneth P. *Political Socialization*. New York: Oxford University Press, 1969.
Langton, Kenneth P. and M. Kent Jennings. "Political Socialization and the High School Civics Curriculum," *American Political Science Review* 62 (1968); 852–868.
Lewin, Kurt. *Resolving Social Conflicts; Selected Papers on Group Dynamics*. New York: Harper and Row, 1948.
Lewin, K; R. Lippitt and R. White. "Patterns of Aggressive Behavior in Experimentally Created 'Social Climates.'" *Journal of Social Psychology* 10 (1939): 271–299.
Lipset, Seymour M. *Political Man. The Social Bases of Politics*. Garden City, N.Y.: Doubleday and Co., 1960.
Lipset, Seymour M. and Earl Raab. *The Politics of Unreason; Right Wing Extremism in America, 1790–1970*. New York: Harper and Row, 1970.
Litt, Edgar. "Civic Education, Community Norms, and Political Indoctrination." *American Sociological Reveiw* 28 (1963): 69–75.

McClosky, Herbert. "Consensus and Ideology in American Politics." *American Political Science Review* 58 (1964): 361—382.

McClosky, Herbert, et al. "Issue Conflict and Consensus Among Party Leaders and Followers." *American Political Science Review* 54 (1960): 406—427.

McDill, Edward L. and Leo C. Rigsby. *Structure and Process in Secondary Schools: The Impact of Educational Climates.* Baltimore: Johns Hopkins University Press, 1973.

Medley, D.M. and H.E. Mitzel. "A Technique for Measuring Classroom Behavior." *Journal of Educational Psychology* 49 (1958): 86—92.

Merton, Robert K. and Alice Kitt. "Contributions to the Theory of Reference Group Behavior." In Robert K. Merton and Paul F. Lazarsfeld (eds.), *Continuities in Social Research: Studies in the Scope and Method of "The American Soldier."* Glencoe, Ill.: The Free Press, 1950, pp. 40—105.

Meyer, John W. "The Charter: Conditions of Diffuse Socialization in Schools." W.R. Scott, (ed.), *Social Processes and Social Structures.* New York: Holt, 1970.

Mill, John Stuart. *On Liberty.* Boston: Atlantic Monthly Press, 1921.

Minuchin, Patricia; B. Biber; E. Shapiro and L. Zimiles. *The Psychological Impact of School Experience: A Comparative Study of Nine-Year-Old-Children in Contrasting Schools.* New York: Basic Books, 1969.

Moos, Rudolf H. "Conceptualizations of Human Environments." *American Psychologist* 28, no. 8 (1973a): 652—664.

— "Conceptualizing Educational Environments." Southeast Asia Development Advisory Group Paper, 73—6, 1973b.

— *The Social Climate Scales: An Overview.* Palo Alto, Calif.: Consulting Psychologists Press, Inc., 1974.

Moos, Rudolf H. and Evelyn Bromet. "The Relation of Patient Attributes to Perceptions of the Treatment Environment." Manuscript, Social Ecology Laboratory, Stanford University, 1976.

Nielsen, H. Dean and Diana H. Kirk. "Classroom Climates." In H.J. Walberg (ed.), *Evaluating Educational Performance.* Berkeley: McCutchan, 1974.

— "Learning Environments and Learning Outcomes." Southeast Asia Development Advisory Group Paper, 73—9, 1973.

OECD, *Reviews of National Policies for Education: Germany.* Paris, 1973.

Oppenheim, A.N. and Judith V. Torney. *The Measurement of Children's Civic Attitudes in Different Nations.* IEA Monograph Studies No. 2, Stockholm: Almqvist and Wiksell, 1974.

Pace, Robert and George G. Stern. "An Approach to the Measurement of Psychological Characteristics of College Environments." *Journal of Educational Psychology* 49 (1958): 269—77.

Patrick, John J. *Political Socialization of American Youth: Implementations for Secondary School Social Studies.* Washington, D.C.: National Council for the Social Studies, 1967.

Peaker, Gilbert F. *An Empirical Study of Education in Twenty-One Countries: A Technical Report.* Stockholm: Almqvist and Wiksell and New York: John Wiley, 1975.

Pervin, L.A. "The College as a Social System: Student Perception of Students, Faculty and Administration." *Journal of Educational Research* 61 (1968): 281—284.

Prewitt, Kenneth, assisted by Joseph Okello-Oculi. "Political Socialization and

Political Education in New Nations," in Roberta S. Sigel (ed.) *Learning About Politics*. New York: Random House, 1970.

Prothro, James W. and Charles M. Grigg. "Fundamental Principles of Democracy: Bases of Agreement and Disagreement." *Journal of Politics* 22 (1960): 276–294.

Przeworski, Adam and Henry Teune. *The Logic of Comparative Social Inquiry*. New York: Wiley-Interscience, 1970.

Remmers, H.H. (ed.) *Anti-Democratic Attitudes in American Schools*. Chicago: Northwestern University Press, 1963.

Robinsohn, S.B. and J.C. Kuhlmann, "Two Decades of Non-Reform in West German Education," *Comparative Education Review* 11, no. 3 (1967).

Robinson, W.S. "Ecological Correlations and Behaviors of Individuals." *American Sociological Review* 15 (1950): 351–357.

Rokeach, Milton. *The Open and Closed Mind*. New York: Basic Books, 1960.

Schattschneider, E.E. *The Semi-Sovereign Peoples*. New York: Holt, Rinehart and Winston, 1960.

Schwartzman, Simon "Desenvolvimento e Abertura Politica," *Dados* (1969): 24–56.

Schwille, John. "Predictors of Between-Student Differences in Civics Cognitive Achievement." In Torney, Oppenheim and Farnen (eds.) *Civic Education in Ten Countries*. Stockholm: Almqvist and Wiksell, and New York: John Wiley, 1975.

Selznick, Gertrude and Stephen Steinberg. *The Tenacity of Prejudice*. New York: Harper and Row, 1969.

Sewell, William H. and Vimal P. Shah. "Parents' Education and Children's Educational Aspirations and Achievements." *American Sociological Review* 33, no. 2 (1968): 191–209.

Siegel, L. and L.C. Siegel. "The Instructional Gestalt." In L. Siegel (ed.), *Instruction: Some Contemporary Viewpoints*. San Francisco: Chandler Publishing, 1967.

Sniderman, Paul M. *Personality and Democratic Politics*. Berkeley: University of California Press, 1974.

Sontheimer, Kurt. *The Government and Politics of West Germany*. Translated by Fleur Donecker. London: Hutchison, 1972.

Smith, T.V. and Eduard C. Lindeman. *The Democratic Way of Life*. New York: Mentor, 1951.

Steele, J.M.; E.R. House and T. Kerins. "An Instrument for Assessing Instructional Climate through Low-Inference Student Judgments." *American Educational Research Journal* 8, no. 3 (1971): 447–466.

Stern, George G. "B=f(p,E)." *Journal of Personality Assessment* 28, no. 2 (1964): 161–168.

Stouffer, Samuel A. *Communism, Conformity and Civil Liberties*. New York: Wiley, 1955.

Thorndike, Robert L. *Reading Comprehension in Fifteen Countries. An Empirical Study*. Stockholm: Almqvist and Wiksell and New York: John Wiley, 1973.

de Toqueville, Alexis. *Democracy in America*. Vol. 1, Phillips Bradley (ed.). New York: Vintage Books, 1945.

Torney, Judith V.; A.N. Oppenheim and R.F. Farnen. *Civic Education in Ten Countries. An Empirical Study*. Stockholm: Almqvist and Wiksell, and New York: John Wiley, 1975.

Trickett, Edison J. and Rudolf H. Moos. "Social Environment of Junior High and High School Classrooms." *Journal of Educational Psychology* 65, no. 1 (1973): 93–102.

Tyack, David. "Forming the National Character." *Harvard Educational Review*, Winter, 1966.

Walberg, Herbert J. "The Social Environment as a Mediator of Classroom Learning." *Journal of Educational Psychology* 60 (1969): 443–448.

Walberg, Herbert J. "The Social Environment as a Mediator of Classroom Learning." *Journal of Educational Psychology* 60 (1969): 443–448.

– "Properties of the Achieving Urban Classes." *Journal of Educational Psychology* 60, no. 4 (1972): 381–385.

Weiler, Hans N. "Political Socialization and the Political System: Consensual and Conflictual Linkage Concepts." In Michael W. Kirst (ed.), *State, School and Politics*. Boston: D.C. Heath, 1972.

– "Schools and the Learning of Dissent Norms: A Study of West German Youths." Paper presented at the annual meeting of the American Political Science Association, Chicago, Ill., September, 1971.

– "Some Notes on Education and Political Development." *LACDES, Stanford International Development Education Center, 1973.*

Weiler, Hans N. and David L. Grossman. "Educational Climates and Attitudes Toward Dissent and Violence: A Study of the Political Socialization of Conflict Norms." A Research Proposal, Stanford University, 1973.

Weissberg, Robert. *Political Learning, Political Choice and Democratic Citizenship*. Englewood Cliffs, N.J.: Prentice-Hall, 1974.

Withall, J. "The Development of a Technique for the Measurement of Social-Emotional Climate in Classrooms." *Journal of Experimental Education* 17 (1949): 347–61.

Wittes, Simon. "School Organization and Political Socialization." In Byron G. Massialas (ed.), *Political Youth, Traditional Schools*. Edgewood Cliffs, N.J.: Prentice-Hall, 1972.

Wolf, Richard. "The Measurement of Environments." In Rudolf H. Moos and Paul M. Insel (eds.), *Issues in Social Ecology: Human Milieus*. Palo Alto, Calif.: National Press Books, 1974.

Wrightstone, J.W. "Measuring Teacher Conduct of Class Discussion." *Elementary School Journal* 34 (1934): 454–460.

Zeigler, Harmon and Wayne Peak. "The Political Functions of the Education System." *Sociology of Education* 43 (1970): 115–142.

Zellman, Gail L. and David O. Sears. "Childhood Origins of Tolerance for Dissent." *Journal of Social Issues* 27 (1971): 109–136.